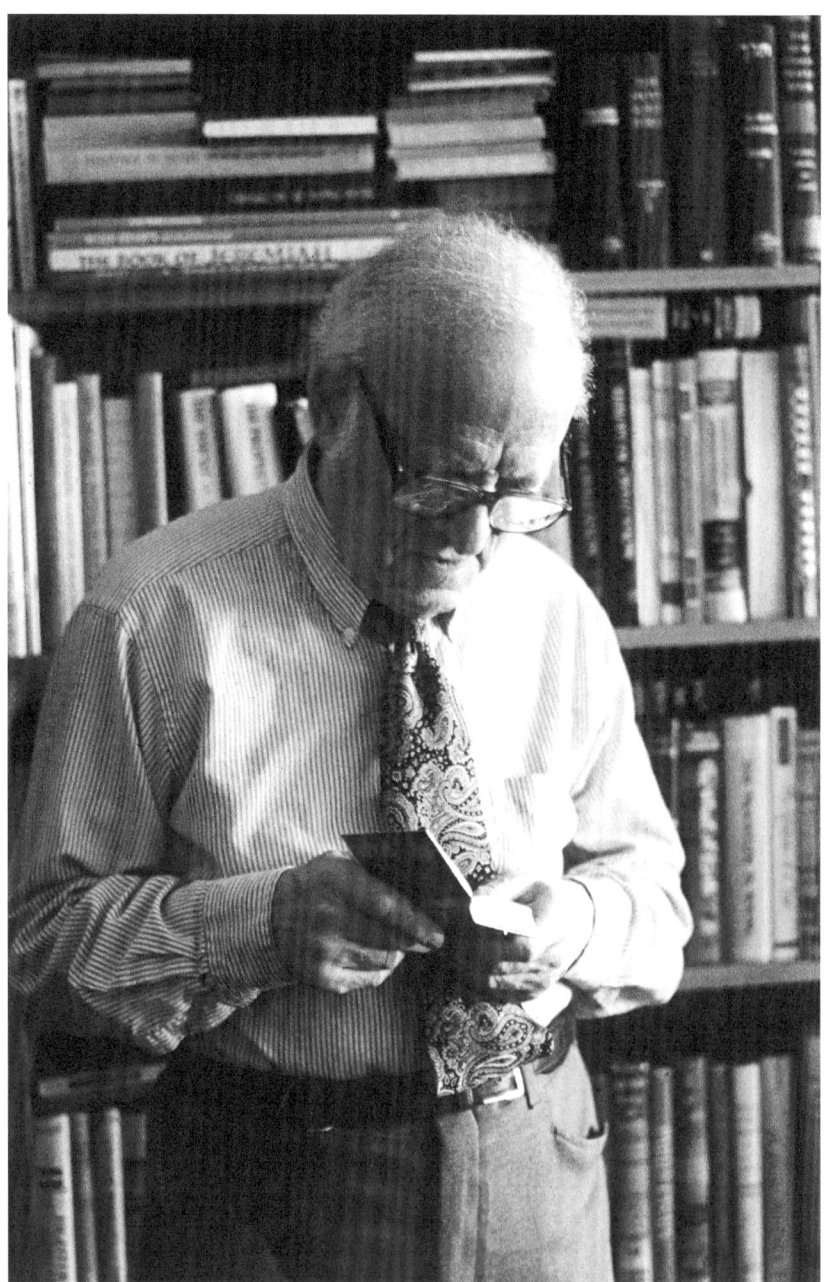

Ismar David with the books he designed, ca. 1985

The Book Jackets
of Ismar David
A Calligraphic Legacy

MISHA BELETSKY

RIT Cary Graphic Arts Press · *Rochester*

The Typophiles · *New York*

2011

ISBN 978-1-933360-51-5

Was du ererbt von deinen Vätern hast, erwirb es,
um es zu besitzen (What you inherited from your
fathers, acquire it to make it become your own)

— Johann Wolfgang von Goethe, *Faust*[1]

WE have come to shy away from absolute qualifiers in this fractured world. To call something *beautiful* seems at best empty and—at worst—pretentious. Yet no other word better suits the book jackets designed by Ismar David, and no other word explains the lasting importance of his work.

Book Jacket Design in the U.S.

Book jacket design originated in Britain in the early nineteenth century[2] as a humble utilitarian object, a wrapper intended to protect the binding of a book. Whereas the book interior and the binding began to receive more attention from publishers by the turn of the twentieth century, as the Arts and Crafts idea of "designing" a book took root, the book jackets showed few signs of artistic involvement for another two decades.

Like other types of packaging by the end of 1920s, the American book jacket had evolved into an independent medium of commercial art. Publishers realized the advertising impact that could be accomplished through an effective use of image, color, and type.

Jacket artists looked for models for this new feature of the book in the old, traditional book elements, such as title page, frontispiece, and binding. Many popular jackets of that period were image-driven in the tradition of the nineteenth-century illustrated book, acting as a glorified frontispiece. Some illustrated jackets drew on the tradition of

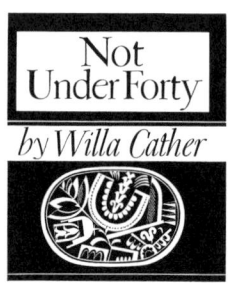

Willa Cather, *Not Under Forty*
Jacket design by
W. A. Dwiggins for
Alfred A. Knopf, 1936

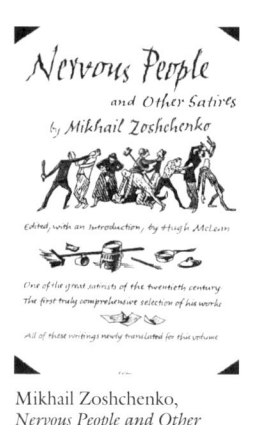

Mikhail Zoshchenko,
*Nervous People and Other
Satires*
Jacket design by
George Salter for
Pantheon Books, 1963

stamped Victorian publishers' bindings, with their extravagant combination of lettering, illustration, and ornament. A few imitated the appearance of the old-fashioned leather binding. Others were more reserved and type-driven, serving as a surrogate title page. Some artists like E. McKnight Kauffer treated the jacket as a miniature poster and created bold, powerful imagery combined with prominent lettering.

Alfred A. Knopf, one of the first trade publishers in the U.S. concerned with the appearance of the interior of the books he published, went out of his way to bring in leading freelance graphic artists like W. A. Dwiggins to design them. Knopf looked down upon the "wrappers" as ephemeral commercial objects. "I'd sooner have good straight twelve-year-old bourbon in a plain and ugly bottle," he wrote, deriding excessive attention to the book jacket.[3] The public at the time agreed. It was common practice to discard the jacket once the book was purchased. For a number of years, the publisher lavished his attention on the interior of the book and its binding, and relegated jackets to the printers. By the early 1930s, Knopf's perfectionism finally led him to pay closer attention to the jackets, as he persuaded Dwiggins to try his hand at jacket design. Dwiggins approached them in his own personal way, using a decorative combination of "simple lettering" with his signature "geometric ornaments" reminiscent of Art Deco combined with Pre-Columbian Mayan motifs and "savage color."[4] The result was at once in keeping with the tradition, yet unlike anything that existed in books before. The genre began to come into its own.

By the late 1930s, German émigré George Salter joined Dwiggins as another important book and jacket designer for Alfred A. Knopf. Other leading publishers also caught on to the potential of this new approach—notably Random House, Little Brown, and Doubleday. Salter brought to the American book jacket his experience from the creatively fertile decade of the Weimar Republic. As one of the most talented and successful artists in the field during this period, he mastered an impressive range of styles and influences, including Expressionism, Modernism, airbrush illustration, and significantly, a full repertoire of calligraphic hands.

The success of Dwiggins and Salter in the 1930s helped to firmly establish calligraphy and lettering as essential to the hallmark look of the American book jacket. From the mid-1930s through the late 1960s, the calligraphic book jacket dominated the scene. According to an estimate made by the calligrapher Charles Skaggs,[5] by the early 1950s, when Ismar David moved to New York, two out of every three book jackets in American bookstores employed calligraphy to some degree. Even the publishers' stationery was often hand-lettered.

Book Jacket Design in Germany

In many ways, the history of German book jacket design parallels the history of its counterpart in the U.S. Both directions have influenced the work of Ismar David.

Bookmaking in Germany, the birthplace of book printing, has always had the highest esteem. German publishers saw the potential of the jacket as a design medium before their American colleagues. Starting from poster-like jackets in the Jugendstil (Art Nouveau style) at the turn of the twentieth century, designers went through a period of vigorous experimentation in the 1920s and 1930s, developing a plethora of styles from Expressionist to Bauhaus Modernist to Art Deco.

Following the twelve years of Nazi domination (1934–45), that were so intolerant to creative expression, designers were once again free to experiment with styles. But in the shell-shocked post-war society it was the classical, purely typographic and calligraphic style that held the greatest appeal. The German reading public was accustomed to this style through the work of E. R. Weiss, Walter Tiemann, and

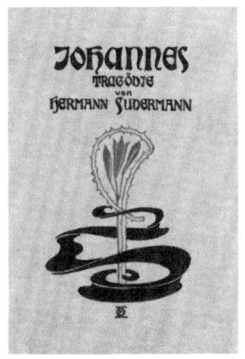

Hermann Sudermann, *Johannes*
Jacket design by
Otto Eckmann, 1899

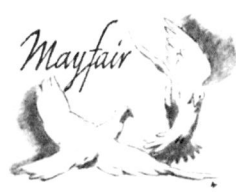

Michael Arlen, *Mayfair*
Jacket design by
E.R. Weiss, 1930

7

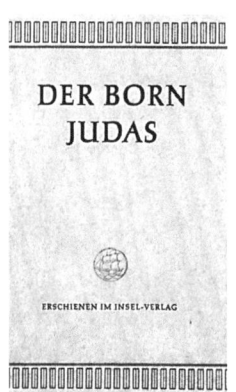

Micha Josef Berdyczewski,
Emanuel Berdyczewski,
Rahel Ramberg, *Der Born Judas*
Jacket design by
Gotthard de Beauclair, 1959

The Golden Book
Cover design for
Keren Kayemet L'Yisrael by
Ismar David, 1938

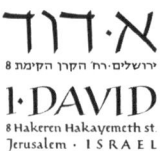

Ismar David's business card,
Jerusalem, Israel, ca.1950

others from the Weimar years. Hermann Zapf, Richard von Sichowsky, and Gotthard de Beauclair emerged as the most successful proponents of this style after the war. In the conservative and conflict-weary German marketplace of the 1950s, the beautiful, dignified and essentially bookish calligraphic cover competed with other calligraphic covers and was not necessarily subject to the usual commercial "survival of the loudest." For a short period, the same could be said of the American marketplace.

Enter Ismar David

Ismar David was born in Breslau, Germany, in 1910 and educated at Städtische Kunstgewerbe- und Handwerkerschule Berlin (Berlin's Municipal School for Arts and Crafts). Calligrapher Johannes Boehland was among his teachers there.

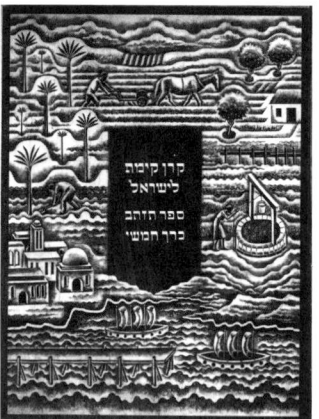

In 1932, David won an international competition for a cover design for Keren Kayemet's (Jewish National Fund) *The Golden Book*, essentially a binder of donor certificates. David was eager to get out of Germany and jumped at the opportunity to leave the country for Palestine in order to supervise the book's production. His first book cover not only marked the beginning of his professional career as a designer, but also indirectly saved his life, as he left the year before Hitler came to power.

He established himself as a graphic artist in the small world of the *Yishuv*, the pre-independence Jewish community. At the time, the Jewish-owned institutions and industry in Palestine were at their embryonic stage. Good typesetting was rare and printing was primitive. This environment

8

proved advantageous to the young artist, who was called upon to design identity programs for companies that would grow to become some of the largest in the country.

He designed their advertisements, publications, and packaging. After the independence of Israel was declared in 1948, David was commissioned to design currency, postage stamps, and state symbols.

Logo for the Carmel Wine Company, ca. 1950

The variety and scope of work called for creative versatility. Due to the lack of available types, the artist had to hone his lettering skills and develop a range of lettering styles.

The same scarcity of good quality Hebrew type compelled David to embark on his quest to create a new typeface. His work began in 1937 and culminated in the 1954 release of David Hebrew by Intertype Corporation in Brooklyn, N.Y.

David's groundbreaking design was not a revival of an existing type, but was inspired by historic calligraphic hands, distilled to their purest expression. David Hebrew went on to become one of today's most popular Hebrew typefaces and may well be considered Ismar David's most recognized legacy in design. Its success may be attributed to the innovative design approach, but more likely it is due to its clarity, grace, and beauty. These same qualities featured prominently in David's jacket design work.

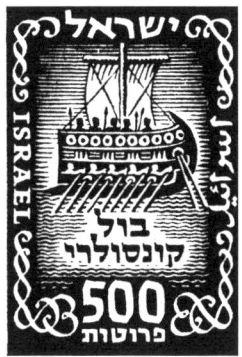

Ismar David's rendering for a trilingual postage stamp design, ca. 1950

Ismar David's freelance commissions with Israeli trade shows brought him to New York on several occasions between 1939 and 1952. On his first visit, he was able to interest Intertype in production of his Hebrew type. After World War II, Dr. Robert Leslie, the owner of The Composing Room typesetting service, acted as an intermediary in the negotiations between David and Intertype. The connection with The Composing Room came to play an important part in David's life, since during his 1952 visit, he decided to marry its publicity director Hortense Mendel and settle in New York City.

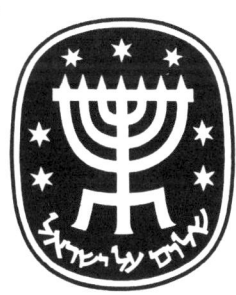

Design proposal by Ismar David and Yerachmiel Schechter for the emblem of the State of Israel, ca. 1950

9

אבגדהוזחטיכל
מנסעפצקרשת־
דסוףץ;:?!][()"'

It would be hard to imagine a better way for a professional designer to arrive in a new country. The Composing Room, together with its public gallery space, was a veritable hub of important happenings in the world of American graphic design. With the help of Hortense Mendel, Dr. Leslie hosted exhibitions of talented young designers in his A-D Gallery, the first gallery in New York devoted to typography and the graphic arts (the name was later changed to Gallery 303). He also publicized their work in *PM* magazine (re-named *A-D)* which he began after the demise of the German graphic arts magazine *Gebrauchsgraphik* in 1934. Dr. Leslie's shows and publications helped jump-start a number of important American careers for the many new arrivals from Europe, including George Salter, Fritz Kredel, Ladislav Sutnar, Herbert Matter, E. McKnight Kauffer, György Kepes, and Jean Carlu. He also encouraged a number of promising young Modernist American designers including Alvin Lustig, Alex Steinweiss, Lester Beall, Will Burtin, and Paul Rand.

In the 1960s, Gallery 303 hosted "Heritage of the Graphic Arts," arguably one of the most comprehensive lecture series on typography and printing in the twentieth century. For nearly two decades Dr. Leslie also served as the president of The Typophiles, the venerable New York organization of traditional book and typography aficionados and the co-publisher of the present volume.

Prior to David's arrival in the U.S., an exhibition of his design work was arranged at the Jewish Museum in New York. Similar to the exhibition at Columbia University that paved the way for the New York arrival of his friend George Salter, this show helped David to establish a name for himself. His wife Hortense, who co-edited *PM* magazine, helped introduce David to art directors at many publishing houses. He arrived as a fully developed artist with a strong portfolio of work he had done previously in Israel. Art directors were duly impressed by the range and quality of his work, and in short order commissions started rolling in for him.

Within a year, David was quite busy working on over thirty jackets for book publishers from Philadelphia to Boston. He entered a fast-paced freelance world, where the sketches were expected within a week, and final camera-ready artwork had to be delivered as hand-separated mechanicals mounted on boards in the course of another week. The rendering of the full-color sketches or comps (an advertising term, adopted by the publishers in the 1950s) often required more time than the final artwork.

When the publisher was located out of town, the week included two or three days of shipping each way, often resulting in designs expected to be completed overnight. Any

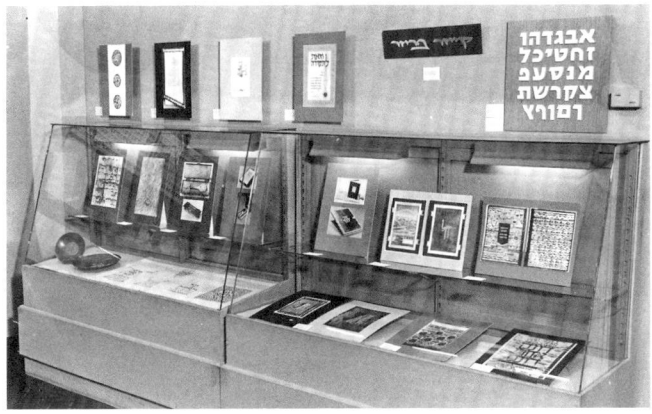

Showcase display of Ismar David's lettering work at the 1953 exhibition, Jewish Museum, New York, NY

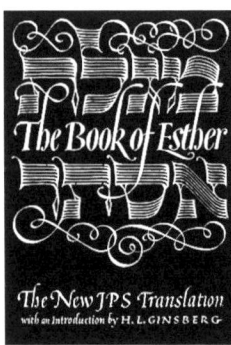

Book of Esther
Cover comp by Ismar David,
1961

changes or corrections called for a revised mechanical, where elements of the design needed to be lifted from the overlays, redone and pasted up anew. This *had* to happen overnight, even for local clients. One finds it difficult to believe all this could be accomplished without the aid of the computer. David's clients were pleased, and the assignments steadily increased.

Unlike George Salter, who recommended David for a teaching position at the Cooper Union (where Salter also taught), David never had a chance to design book jackets in his native Germany. His experience there was basically academic. Consequently, he was less influenced by the un-bridled experimentation of Weimar commercial art. His teaching position stimulated his mastery of a variety of his-toric calligraphic styles. He later mentioned that he wanted to "stay one step ahead of his students."[6] In fact, he became accomplished in dozens of Latin and Hebrew calligraphic styles, as testified by the showings in his respective writing manuals *Our Calligraphic Heritage*, 1979, and *The Hebrew Letter: Calligraphic Variations*, 1990. Traditional calligraphic forms became the basis of his commercial work as well.

David's emerging graphic style was more direct and tra-ditional than either Dwiggins' or Salter's work. Yet it was un-mistakably contemporary and spoke to the public of his time. He strove for "timelessness . . . fused with contemporary form of expression."[7] He was always interested in designing the complete composition and occasionally declined offers for lettering alone to be incorporated into someone else's design. He saw himself as the *auteur* of the whole composition. When one hears him admire the work of the *Book of Kells* craftsmen, one gains insight into his own artistic aspirations: "Each page displays the quality of an exquisite tapestry executed with great skill, rich in texture, full of inventiveness, oblivious to economy and time. The writing is completely integrated with the pictorial part of the book and its illuminations."[8]

Ismar David's images are made from the same stuff as his lettering. His lines are the lines of a calligrapher, and his picture is a perfect companion to his letter—they exist in the same space and are tangible in the same way. His images were developed to the point of becoming a symbol, not unlike a character of a typeface or a logo. "The lines do not define forms, but like the lines of letterforms and other symbols, they have to become symbols themselves. At the same time, they have to form abstract patterns of harmony and be expressive according to the contents of the theme," he asserted.[9]

In contrast to the Modernists like Paul Rand and Alvin Lustig, who gained popularity during the same period, David focused on the expressive power of the letter combined with color and abstract shapes, and not on the concept. His jackets were simple and beautiful, communicating through the sheer visual power of type and color, much in the same way as the best of the post-war German jackets.

David reveled in the challenges of printing processes. He knew printing intimately and prepared artwork not intended for book jackets (such as his 1971 illustrations for the Limited Editions Club publication of Pascal's *Les Pensées*) on overlays, as camera-ready copy. He prided himself on being able to use limited means of printing in two or three inks to achieve maximum effect. At times, his proficiency with the medium was such that he could make a two-color jacket design appear as though it had been printed in full-color.[10]

Ismar David was one of perhaps three dozen calligraphers of that period who established themselves as jacket designers providing accomplished lettering for their jackets. Warren Chappell, Arnold Bank, Phil Grushkin, Hollis Holland, Charles Skaggs, Oscar Ogg, Jeanyee Wong, and Lili Wronker were among the most successful. David's work is distinguished from other work of the period not only as attractive and refined, but also powerful and expressive. His lettering is charged with an extra dimension of emotion.

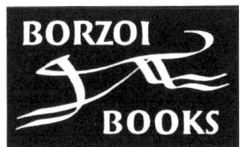

Logo design by Ismar David for Alfred A. Knopf, 1954

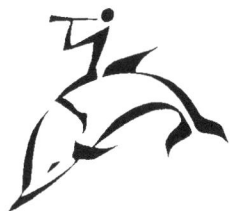

Logo design by Ismar David for Houghton Mifflin, ca. 1960.
This logo is still used by the publisher at this time.

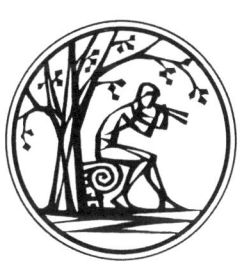

Logo design by Ismar David for Riverside Press, 1964

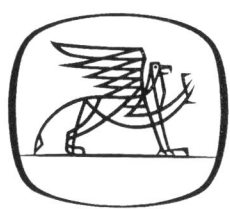

Logo design by Ismar David for Golden Press, ca. 1960

13

He aimed for "the rhythm, pulse, and sensitivity [to be] transmitted through the writing hand."[11] His lettering is elegant and fluent, yet assertive and direct. ". . . I use lines and color . . . to serve my own [expressive] needs and to communicate my ideas and my feelings in the service of the book," he explained.[12]

David regarded calligraphy as a valid means of artistic expression and encouraged his colleagues to take pride in their line of work. "Calligraphy . . . has found its place as a cultural medium alongside the visual arts. And here it is unique as it fuses the timeless principles of art with ancient traditions of crafts," he wrote.[13] His palette included lettering, colors, symbolism, decoration, and abstraction and his canvas was the book jacket. David's goals as an applied artist were much the same as any fine artist's.

Aside from its artistic merits, he ascribed redemptive qualities to calligraphy as a humanizing handicraft, echoing the ideas Eric Gill expressed in his 1931 *Essay on Typography*: "Calligraphy is far from being an anachronism—it is part of the seasoning that makes our fare of industrial culture more palatable."[14]

Title page design by Ismar David for *Our Calligraphic Heritage*, 1979

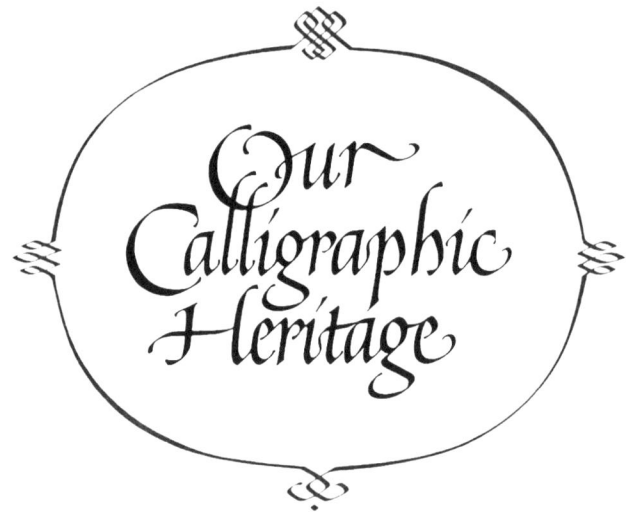

14

By the late 1960s, the graphic fashion had changed. Publishers were no longer interested in calligraphy on their jackets and as a result, the publishing commissions "dried up" for Ismar David and his calligrapher colleagues. They explored other directions. Many turned to teaching. David increasingly focused on architectural design and lettering among other areas of design. His involvement in books continued with several important projects appearing through the 1970s and the 1980s. In addition to *Our Calligraphic Heritage* and *The Hebrew Letter,* the writing manuals he authored and designed, he illustrated and designed a bilingual limited edition of *The Psalms*, which was included in the Fifty Books of the Year selection by the American Institute of Graphic Arts (AIGA) in 1973.

Conclusion

In the ensuing years, one style quickly supplanted another. There were formulaic jackets in the International style, Art Nouveau-inspired psychedelic jackets, eclectic jackets, jackets with the 1970s "big" lettering by the likes of Paul Bacon, and gimmicky photo-typography. There were scores of image-driven illustrated jackets, as if resurrected from the 1920s. As for the majority of them—they were undistinguished. Occasionally, important designers like Milton Glaser and Fred Marcellino contributed an outstanding jacket, but these were exceptions, rather than the rule. Book jackets once again became a second-rate province in the graphic arts.

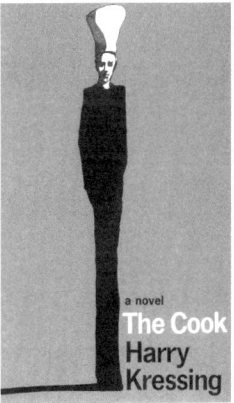

Harry Kressing, *The Cook*
Jacket design by
Milton Glaser, 1965

Things began to change in the late 1970s, when Louise Fili became art director at Pantheon. She employed tactful period typography and decoration and restored some of the lost elegance to book jackets as a genre. A new generation of designers brought to book jackets a new, irreverent aesthetic derived from record cover design and advertising, among other fields. Carin Goldberg began designing jackets for Random House in the early 1980s. Soon after, a group of designers employed by Alfred A. Knopf discovered a graphic idiom similar to that of the Modernists who designed jackets for the same firm some forty years earlier. The young designers preferred photography to illustration, and multi-layered collage to direct storytelling. Their intriguing concepts and offbeat compositions inspired a host of imitators and helped to put jacket design back on the map.

Book jacket design in the U.S. is perhaps more visible than it ever was. As one indication, the authoritative 50 Books competition held annually since 1923 by the AIGA became 50 Books / 50 Covers in 1997, with covers drawing more attention than the books. Thanks to the high-quality work in the field today, we have come to expect the book jacket to be a place of conceptual brilliance, original thought, social commentary and graphic wit.[15] Yet it may be something more: a thing of beauty.

It appears that the current preference for concept-driven jacket design often comes at the expense of formal craftsmanship. It also seems this neglect for typographic and calligraphic form may be a temporary condition. Once the potential of the conceptual approach is exhausted, designers may find themselves revisiting what we inherited from our fathers, in the words of Goethe, not only to regain craftsmanship, but also to "acquire it to make it our own."[16] The calligraphic legacy of Ismar David's jacket design will be there to show us the way.

Calligraphic tailpiece design by Ismar David for *The Psalms*, 1973

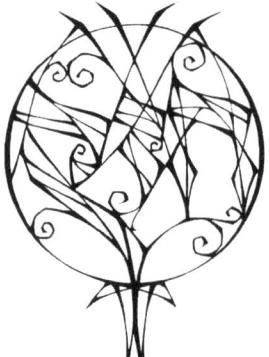

Notes

1. Ismar David, *The Hebrew Letter*, Jason Aronson, 1990, p. 17.

2. Michelle Pauli, "Earliest-known book jacket discovered in Bodleian Library," *The Guardian*, April 24, 2009.

3. Alfred A. Knopf, "A Publisher Looks at Book Design," in *Portrait of the Publisher, 1915–1965*, The Typophiles, 1965, vol. I, p. 88.

4. W. A. Dwiggins, as quoted by Alfred A. Knopf in "Dwig and the Borzoi," *Portrait of the Publisher, 1915–1965*, The Typophiles, 1965, vol. I, p. 113.

5. "American Calligraphy Revisited, 1945–1965," in *Fine Print* 10, 1984.

6. David Pankow, ed., *The Work of Ismar David*, RIT Cary Graphic Arts Press, 2005, p. 11.

7. David Pankow, ed., *The Work of Ismar David*, RIT Cary Graphic Arts Press, 2005, p. 28.

8. Ismar David, *Our Calligraphic Heritage*, Geyer Studio, 1980, p. 11.

9. Ibid.

10. See *A Lost Paradise*, p. 23, for one excellent example.

11. Ismar David, *Our Calligraphic Heritage*, Geyer Studio, 1980, p. 19.

12. David Pankow, ed., *The Work of Ismar David*, RIT Cary Graphic Arts Press, 2005, p. 79.

13. Ismar David, *Our Calligraphic Heritage*, Geyer Studio, 1980, p. 17.

14. Ibid.

15. See "Biblionomatopoeia" by Jessica Helfand, http://observatory.designobserver.com/entry.html?entry=7217.

16. As quoted in Ismar David, *The Hebrew Letter*, Jason Aronson, 1990, p. 17.

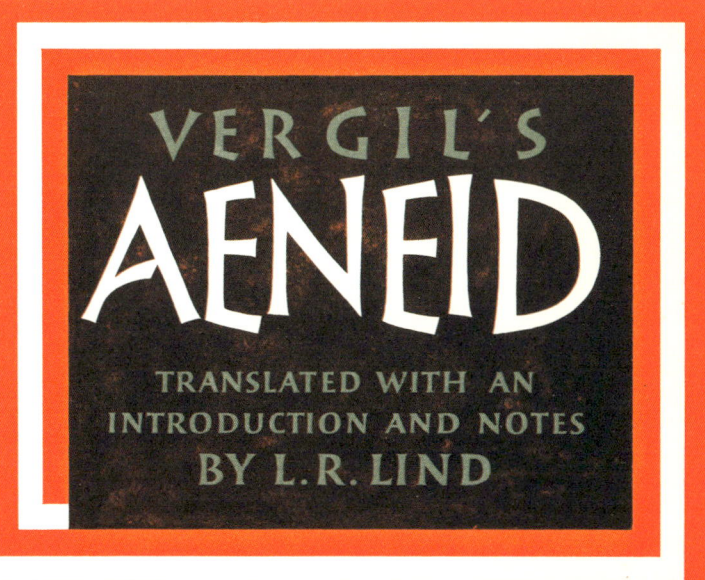

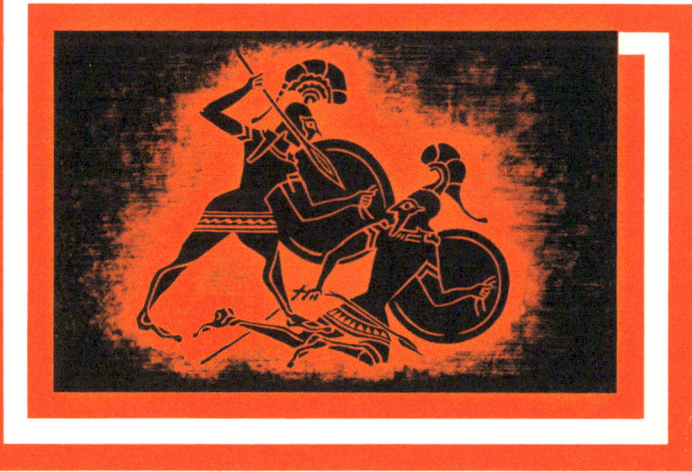

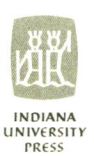

INDIANA
UNIVERSITY
PRESS

MB 45   AN ORIGINAL MIDLAND BOOK / MB 45 / $1.95

A striking design, with the lettering conveying just enough historical flavor to be effective, but no apparent model. The illustrations and ornamentation are based on Greek rather than Roman sources.
INDIANA UNIVERSITY PRESS, 1963

19

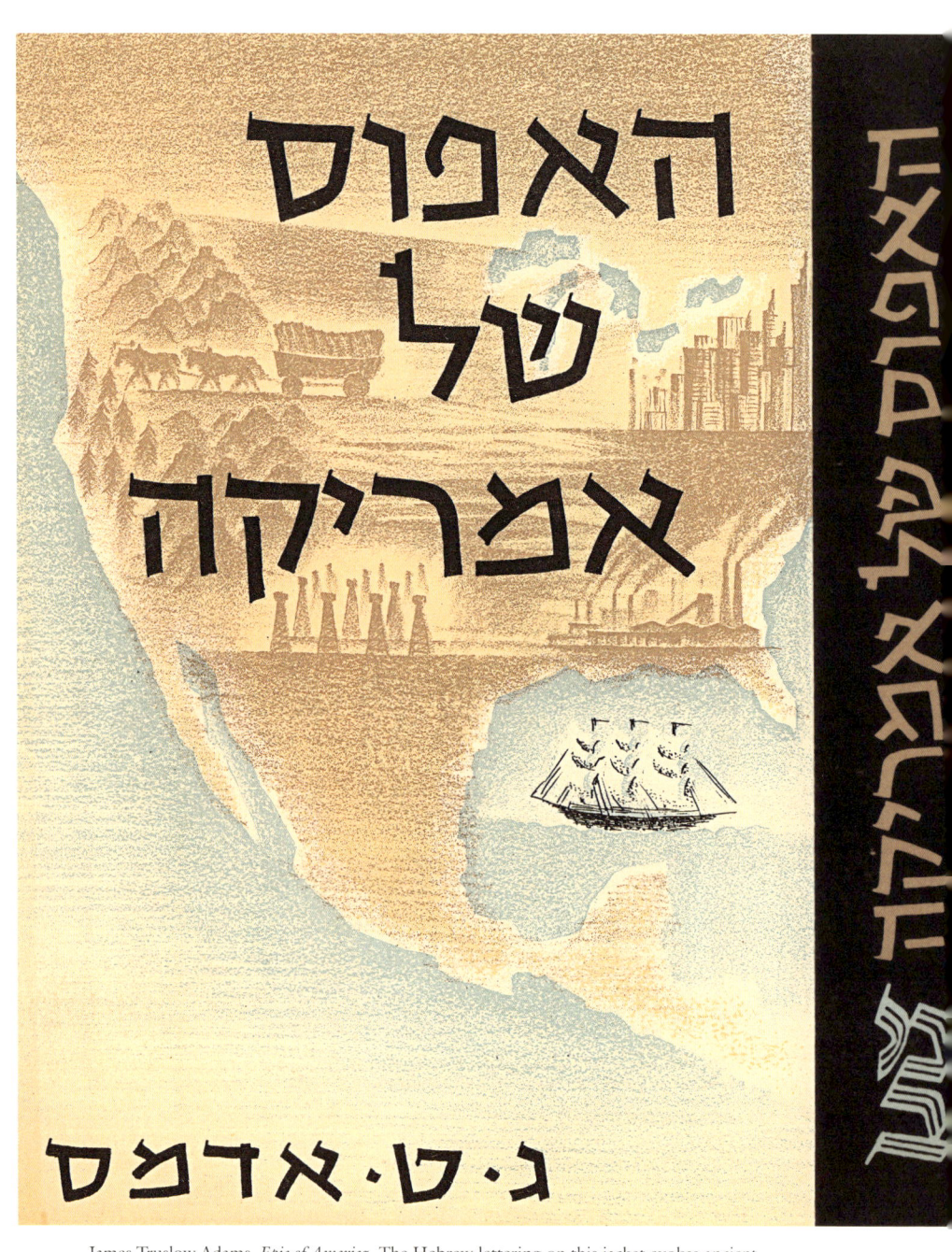

James Truslow Adams. *Epic of America*. The Hebrew lettering on this jacket evokes ancient inscriptions and lends an epic dimension to the design. MOSAD BIALIK, C. 1948

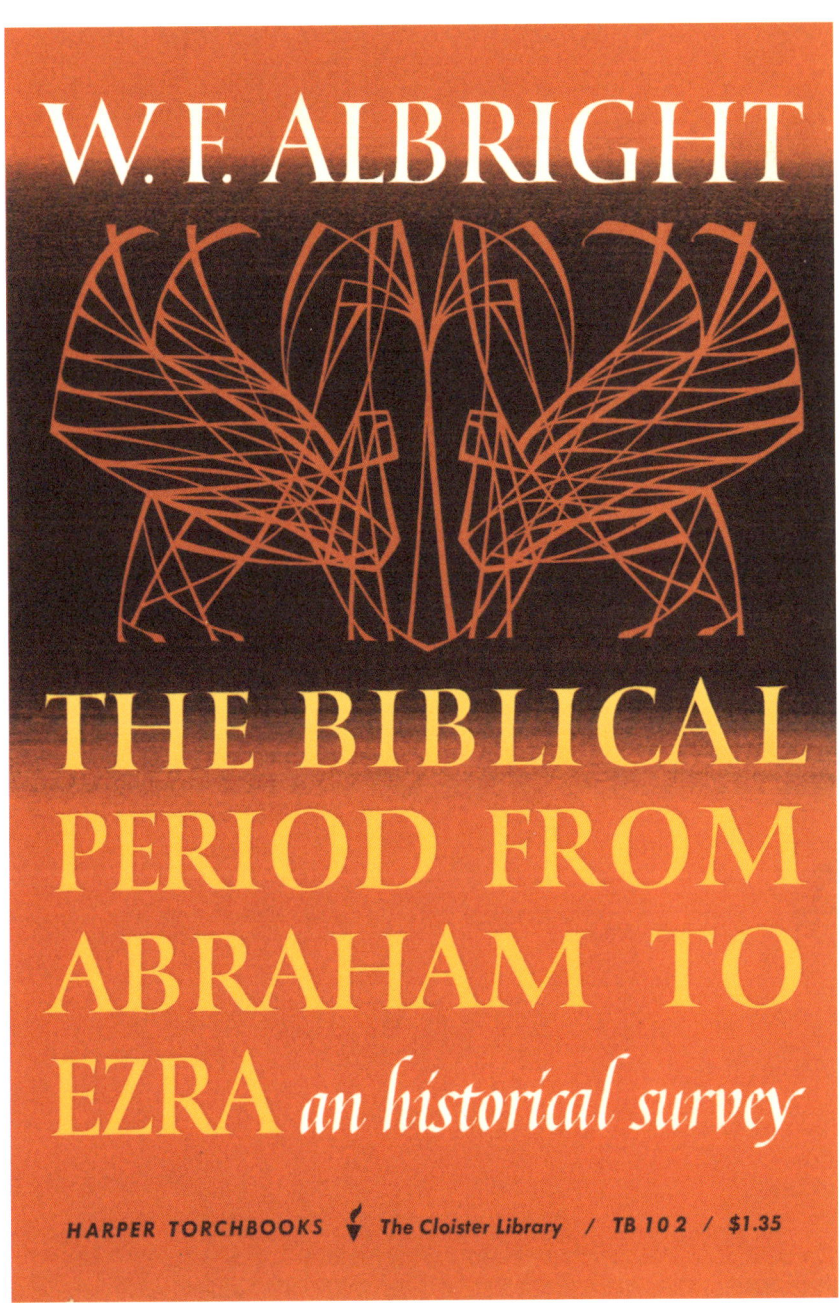

Considering that neither the gryphons nor the Roman lettering style are related directly
to the topic of the book, notice how the combination of color, imagery, and calligraphy succeeds
at expressing just the right feeling of the period. HARPER & ROW, 1963

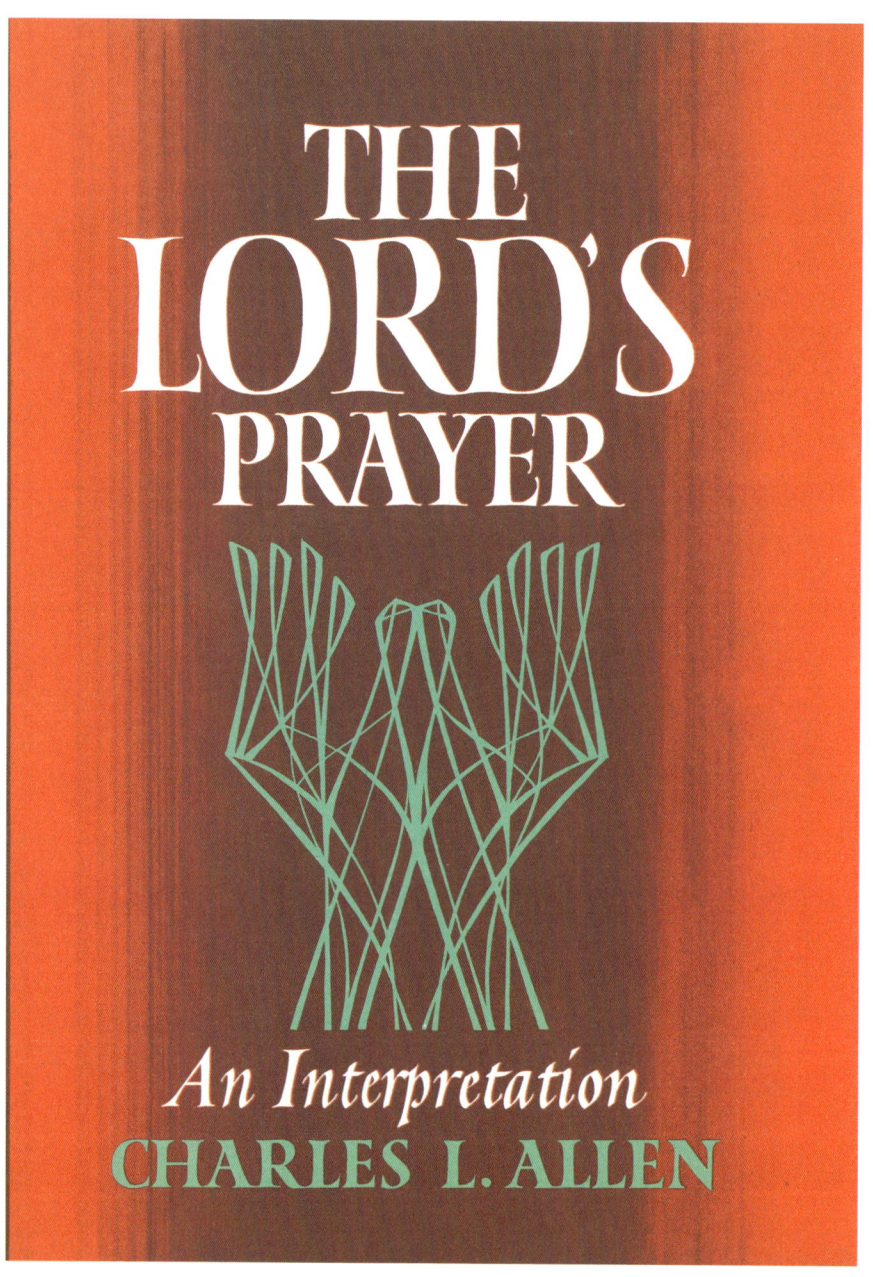

The image and the lettering are in perfect harmony, both created by a single hand in one spirit. Both are integral to the composition, and both are expressive. REVELL, 1963

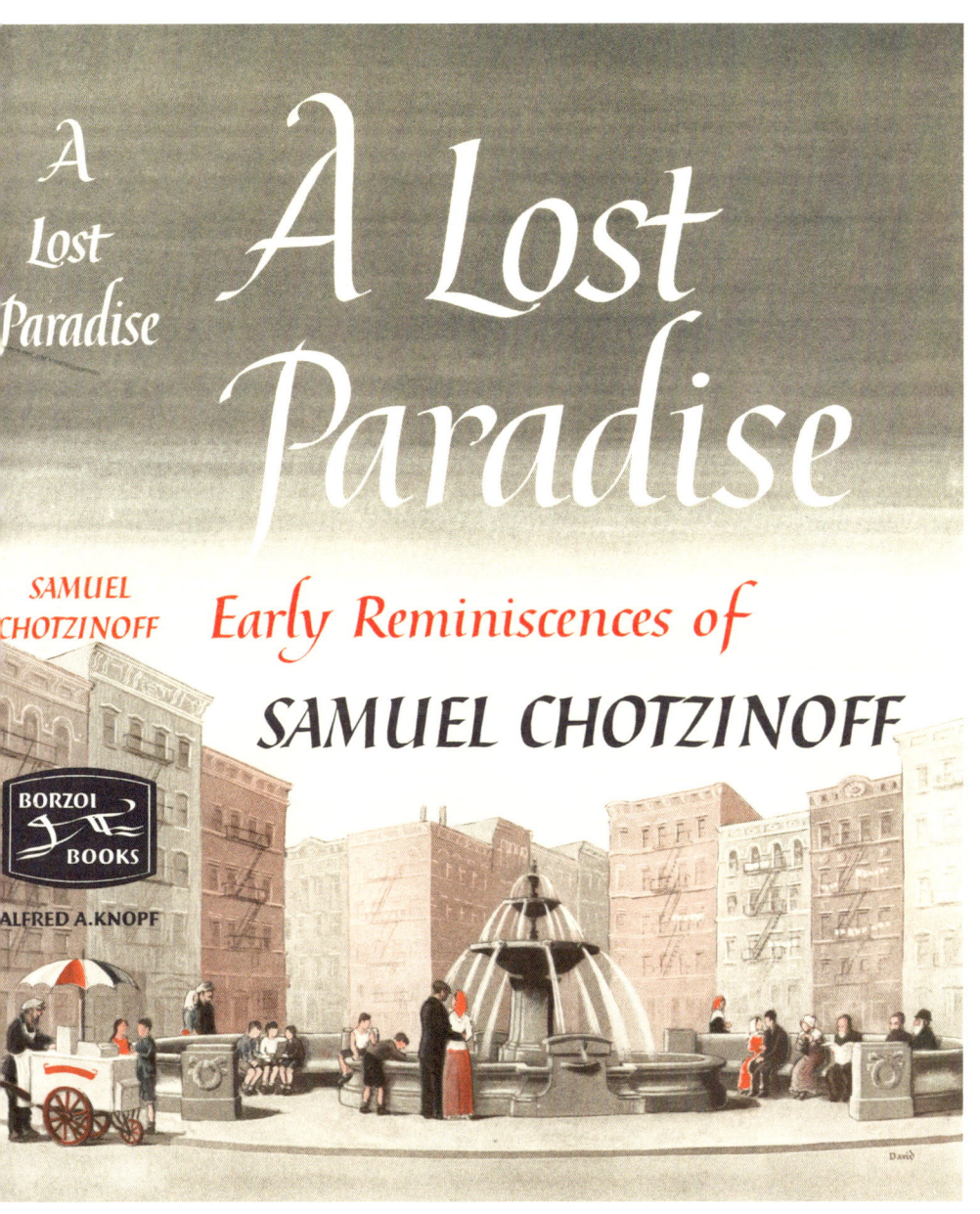

With just two colors at his disposal, the artist creates a faultless illusion of a full-color image. An eerily romantic image with elegant calligraphy seduces the reader with an irresistible sense of nostalgia. KNOPF, 1955

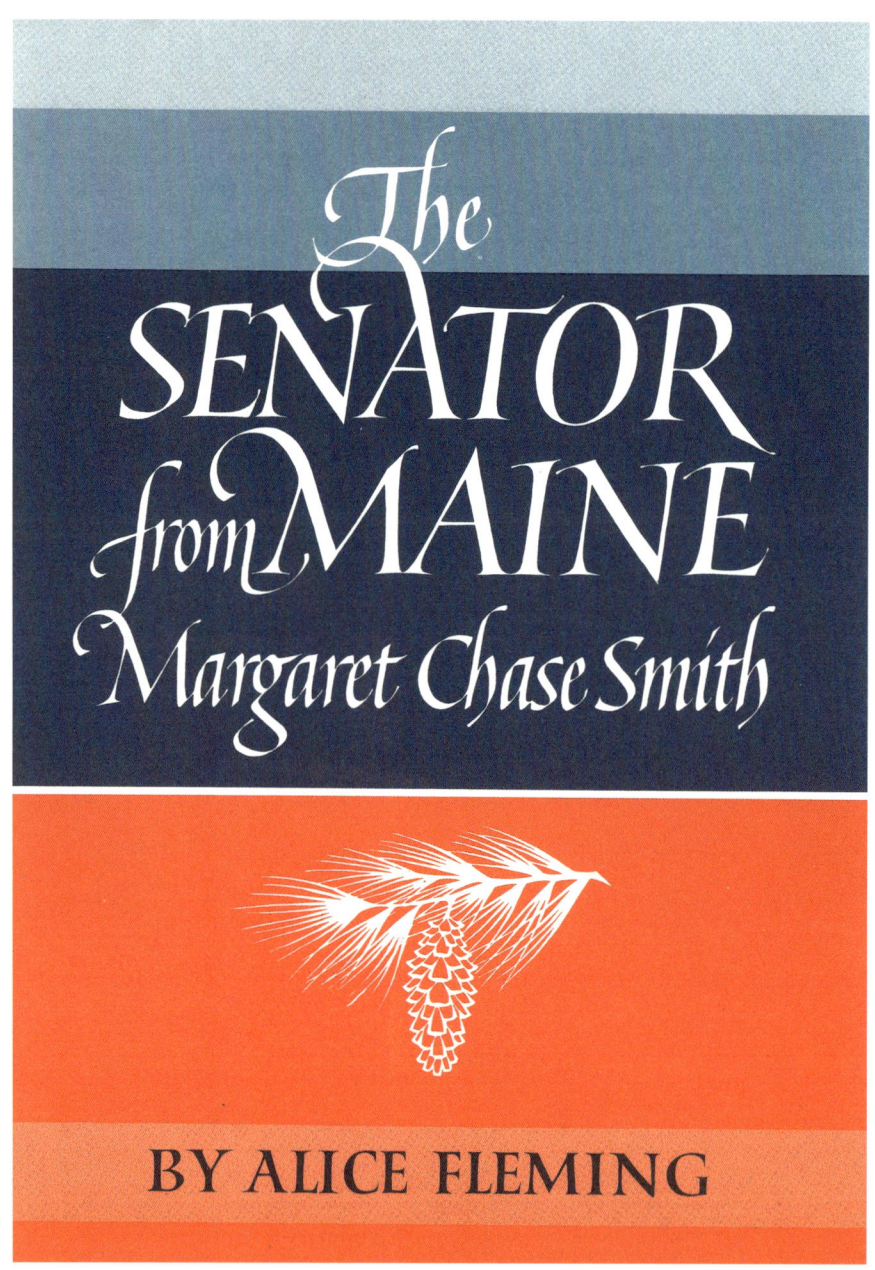

The SENATOR *from* MAINE

Margaret Chase Smith

BY ALICE FLEMING

This subtle exercise in the ubiquitous red, white, and blue election palette proves these colors need not be garish to be effective. CROWELL,1969.

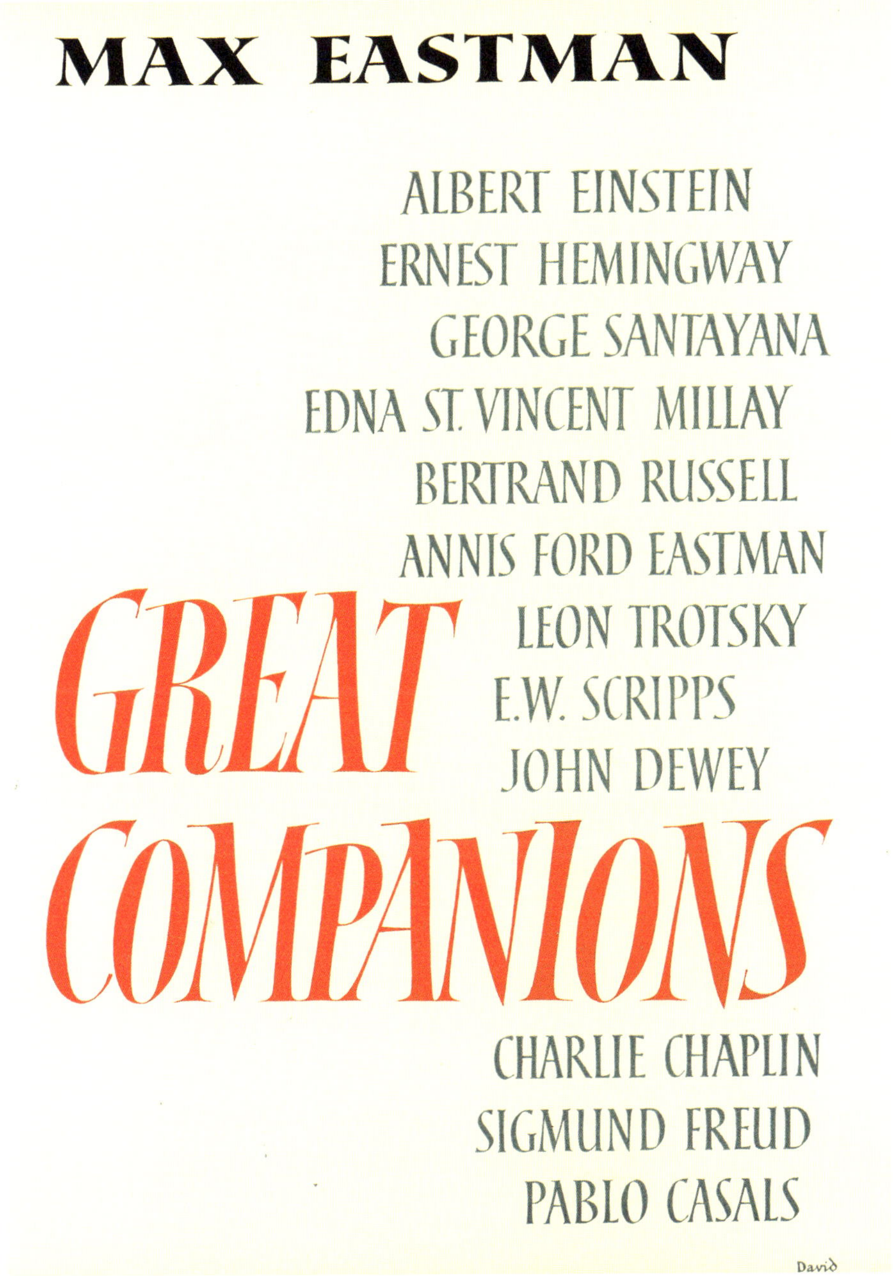

MAX EASTMAN

ALBERT EINSTEIN
ERNEST HEMINGWAY
GEORGE SANTAYANA
EDNA ST. VINCENT MILLAY
BERTRAND RUSSELL
ANNIS FORD EASTMAN
LEON TROTSKY
E.W. SCRIPPS
JOHN DEWEY

GREAT COMPANIONS

CHARLIE CHAPLIN
SIGMUND FREUD
PABLO CASALS

David

A purely calligraphic design which relies on the expressive strength of lettering and the white space alone. FARRAR, STRAUS AND CUDAHY, 1959

25

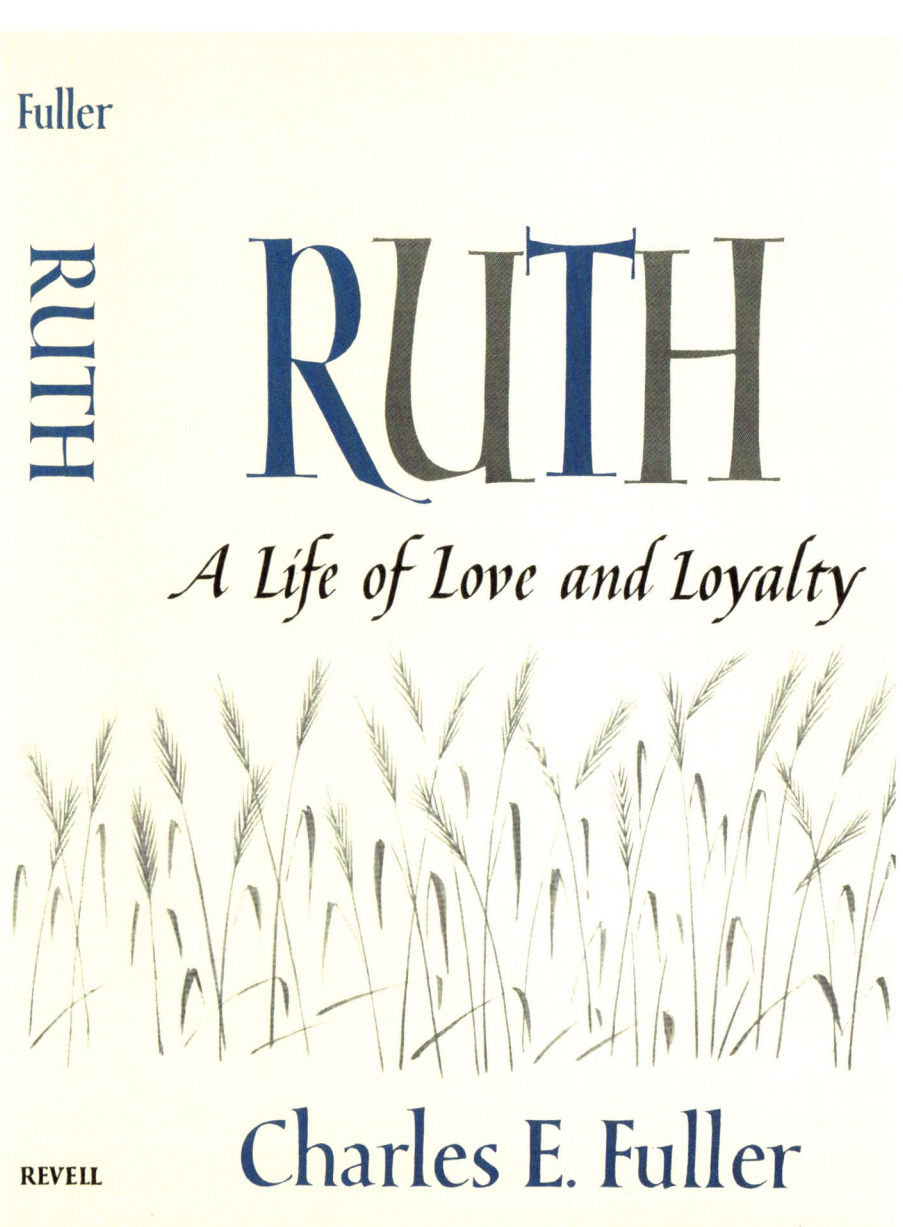

Fuller

RUTH

RUTH

A Life of Love and Loyalty

Charles E. Fuller

REVELL

The playful irregularity and the two-tone coloring of the title lettering, along with the subtle rendering of the illustration, convey a personal approach to the Biblical love story. REVELL, 1959

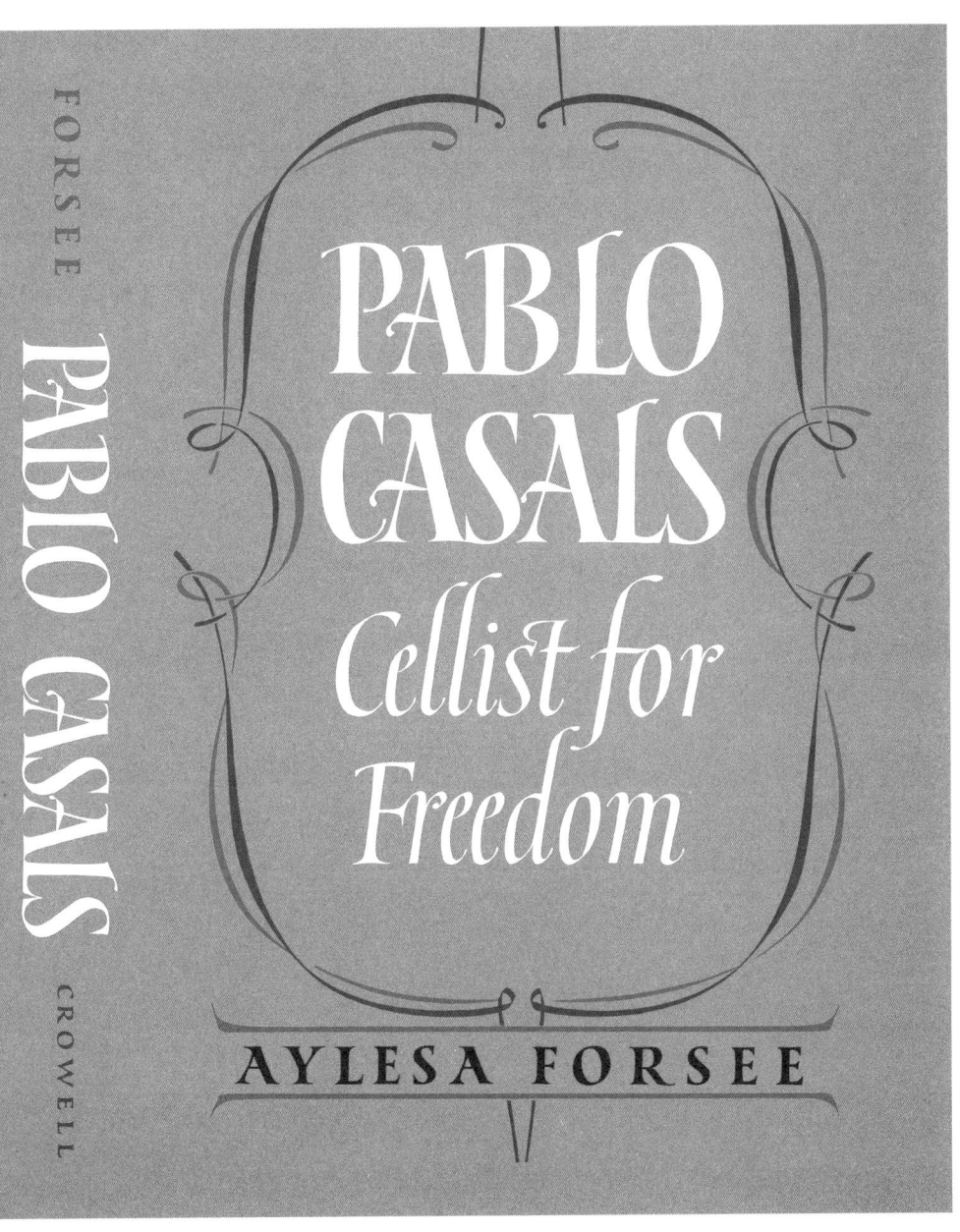

PABLO CASALS
Cellist for Freedom

AYLESA FORSEE

FORSEE

PABLO CASALS

CROWELL

The calligraphic flourishes around the lettering not only form the shape of the cello, but also playfully intertwine to create a visual metaphor for music. The sturdy yet flowing lettering, combined with the dignified colors and balanced symmetrical arrangement, portray the famous performer in abstract visual terms. CROWELL, 1965

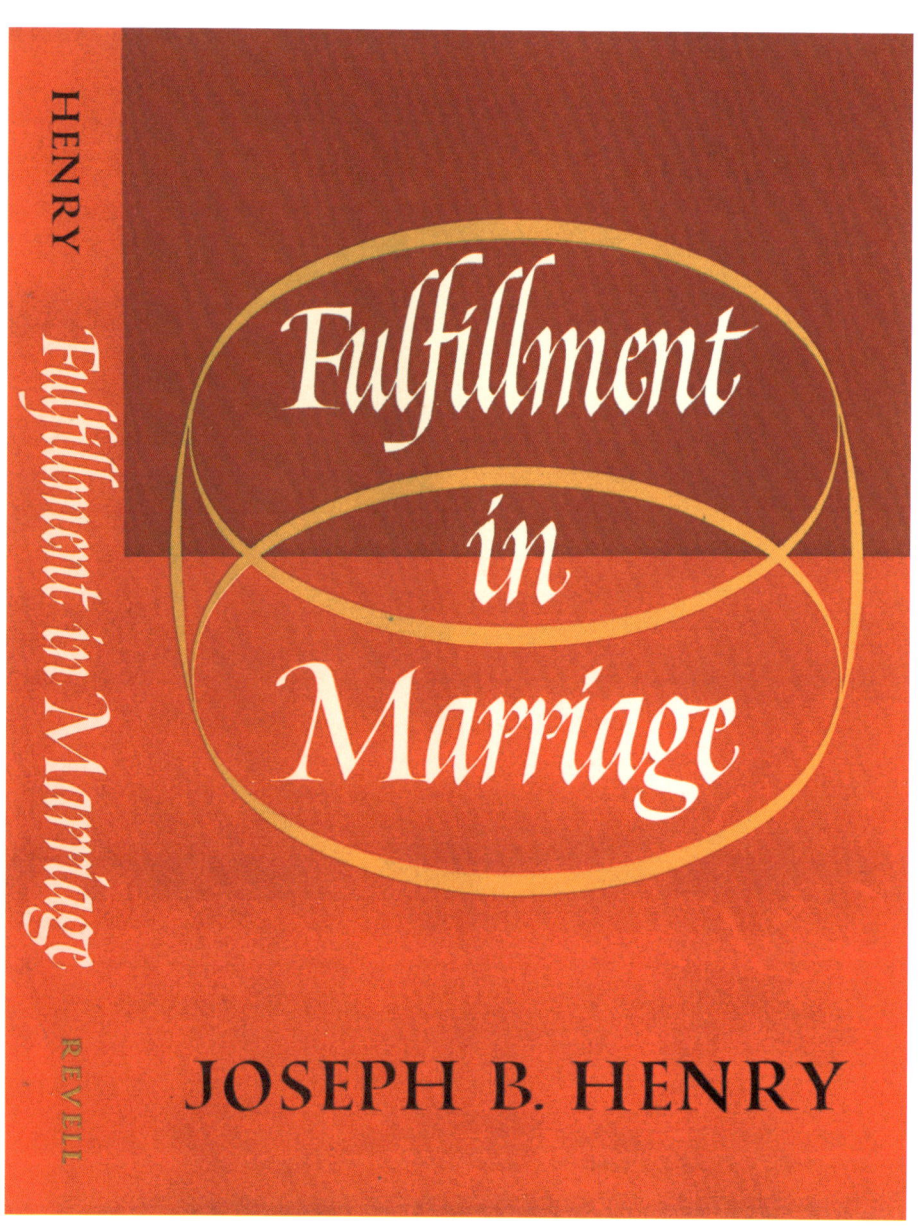

A perfectly balanced composition; the royal yet sensual palette aptly express the subject matter. The circular design represents a wedding band, denotes completion, and binds the title lettering together. REVELL, 1966

28

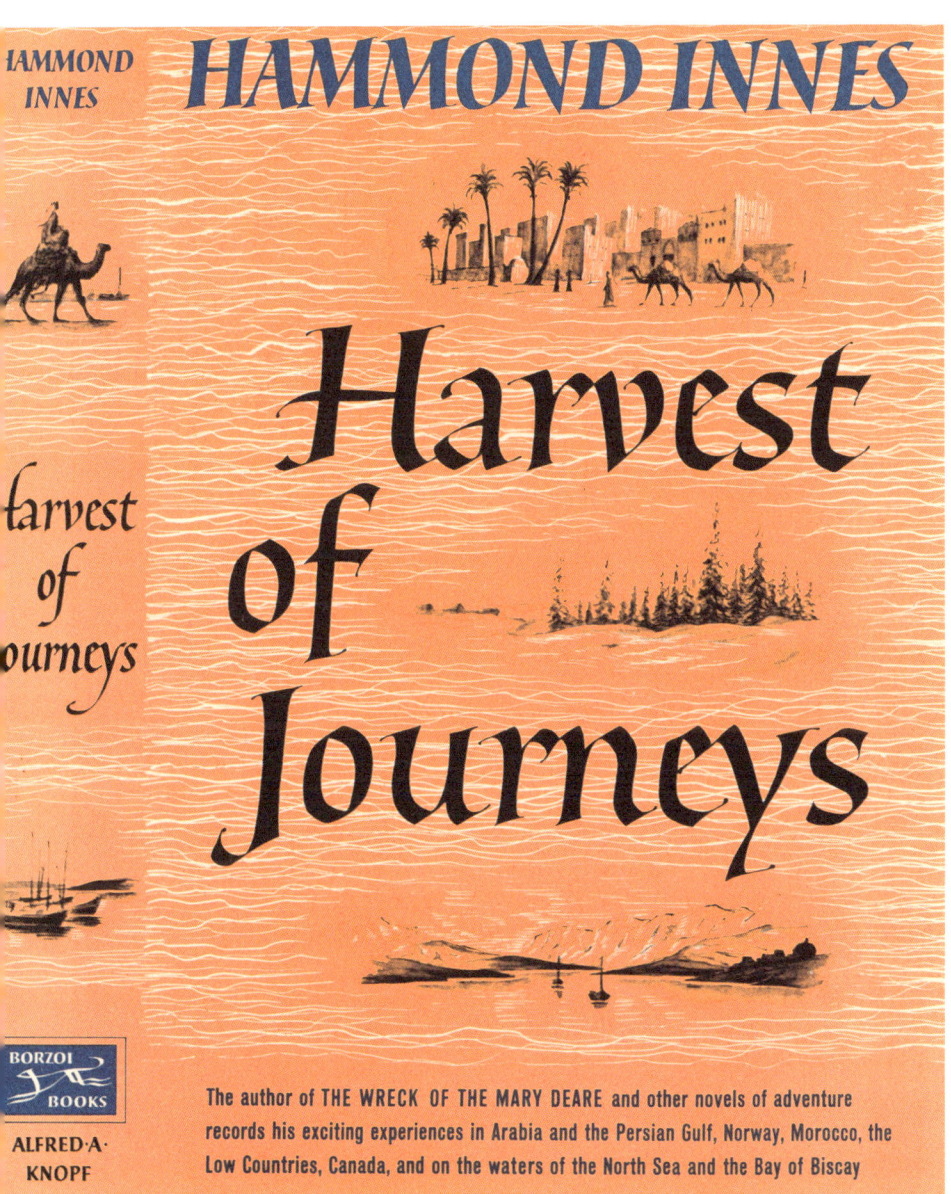

The way in which the evocative illustrations are woven together with the lettering is reminiscent
of George Salter's work. The exotic lettering is unmistakably David's own. KNOPF, 1960

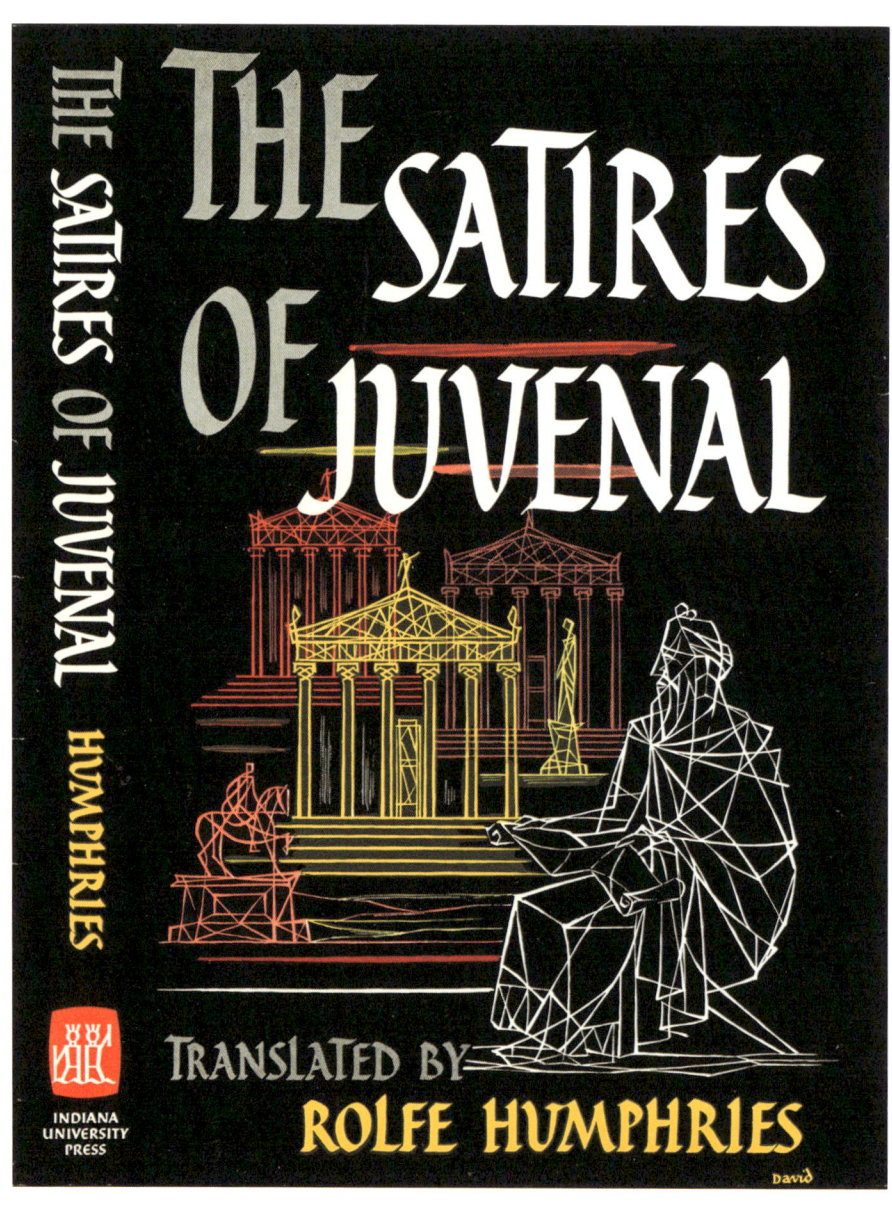

An example of excellent rustic lettering suitable to the period of the text. David's signature calligraphic drawing is superimposed in a distinctly modern fashion. INDIANA UNIVERSITY PRESS, 1958

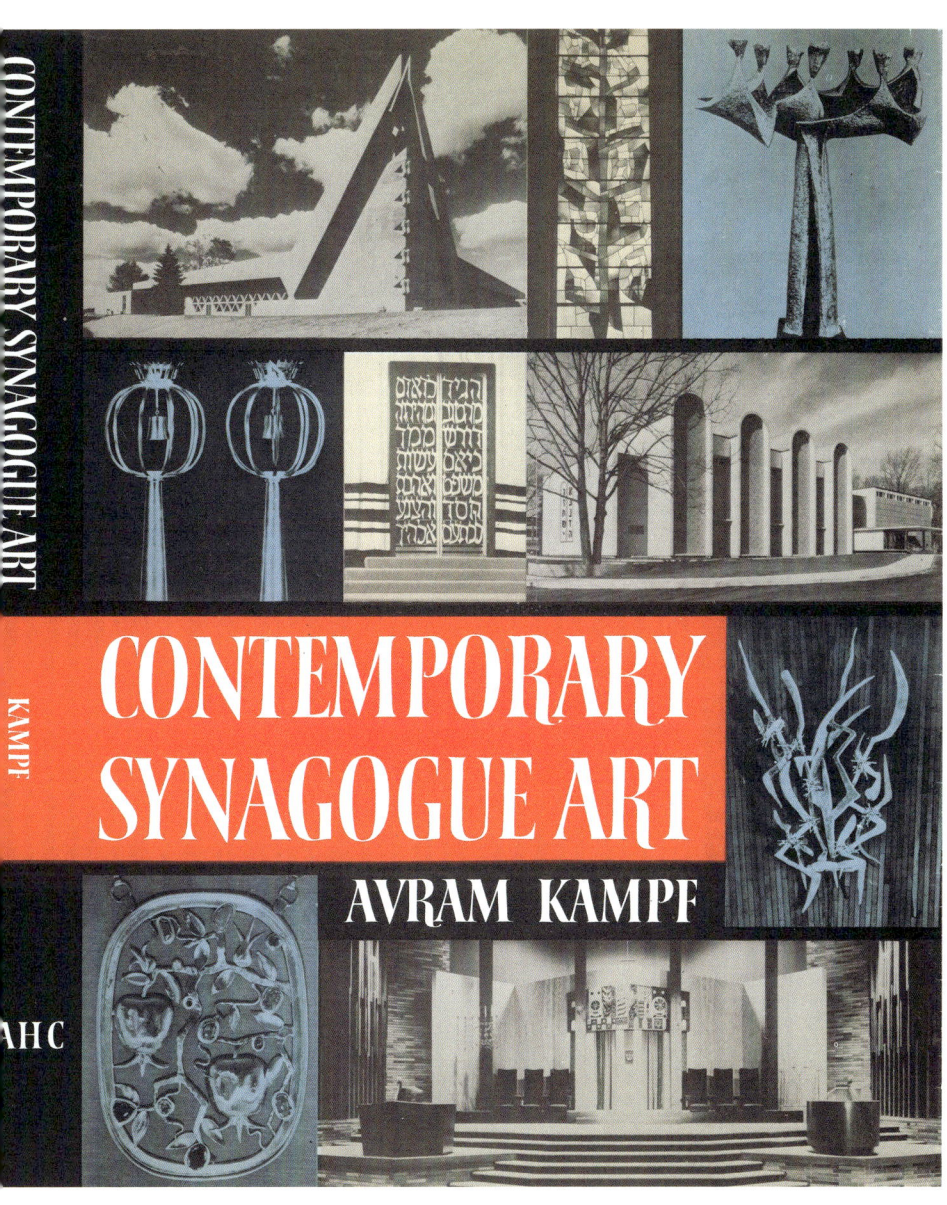

A rare example of David using photography in his jacket design. Modernist rhythmical arrangement of the panels is in contrast with more traditional lettering. UNION OF AMERICAN HEBREW CONGREGATIONS, 1966

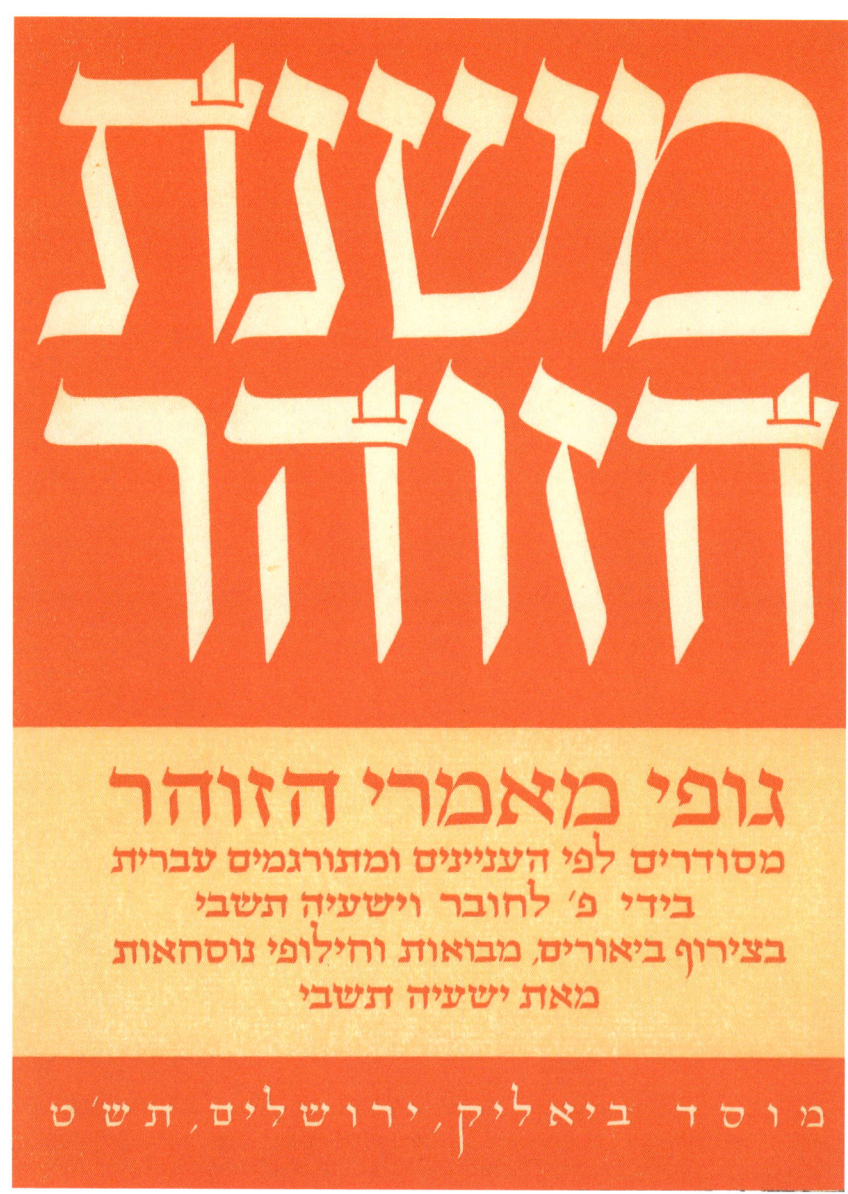

Mishnat ha-Zohar. Arranged and translated by Y. F. Lachower and I. Tishby. A bold calligraphic Hebrew arrangement showing command of historical Sephardi manuscript hands. Division of the front into three panels subtly lends the design a sense of modernity. MOSAD BIALIK, 1949–1961

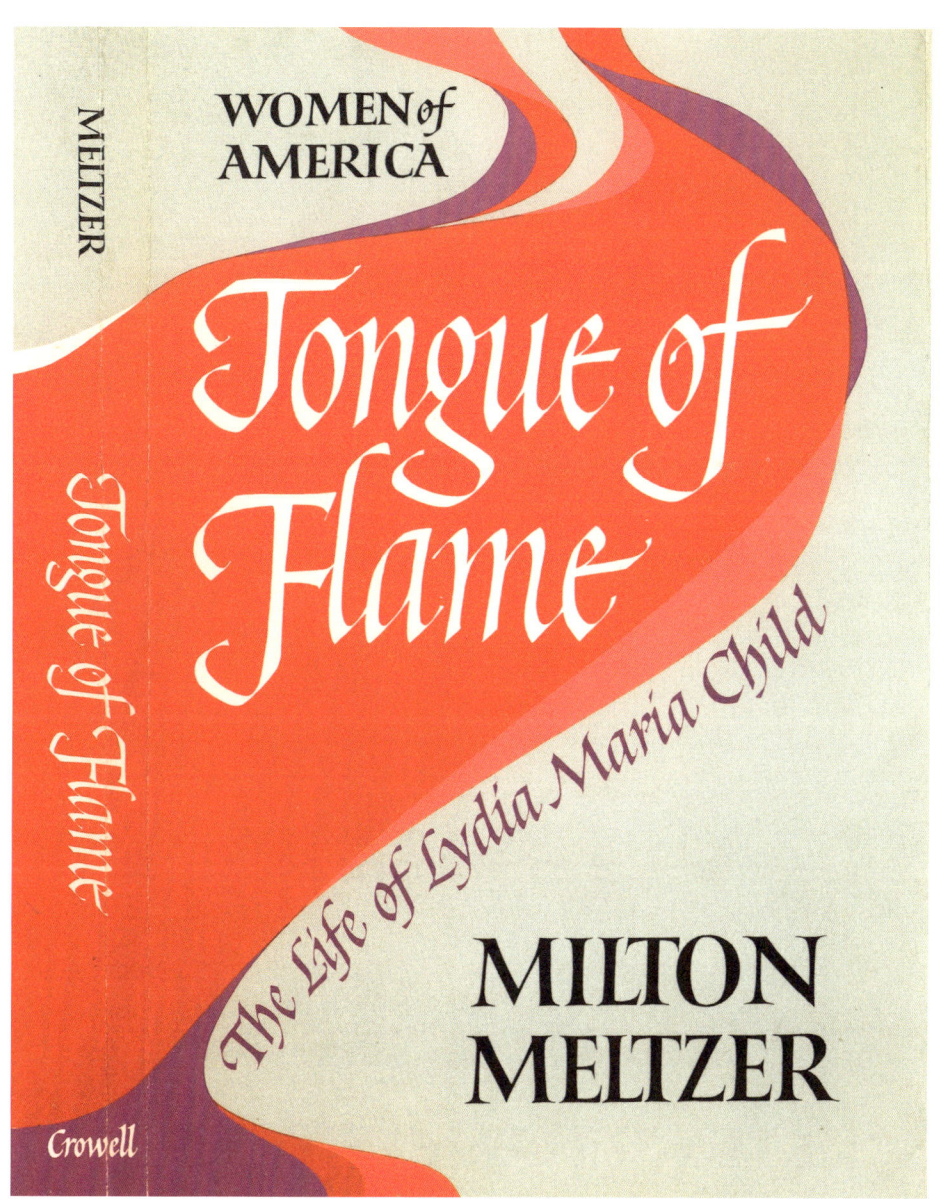

The twisted asymmetrical design does not represent the likeness of a flame, yet combined with edgy lettering, it conveys the burning feeling of danger. CROWELL, 1965

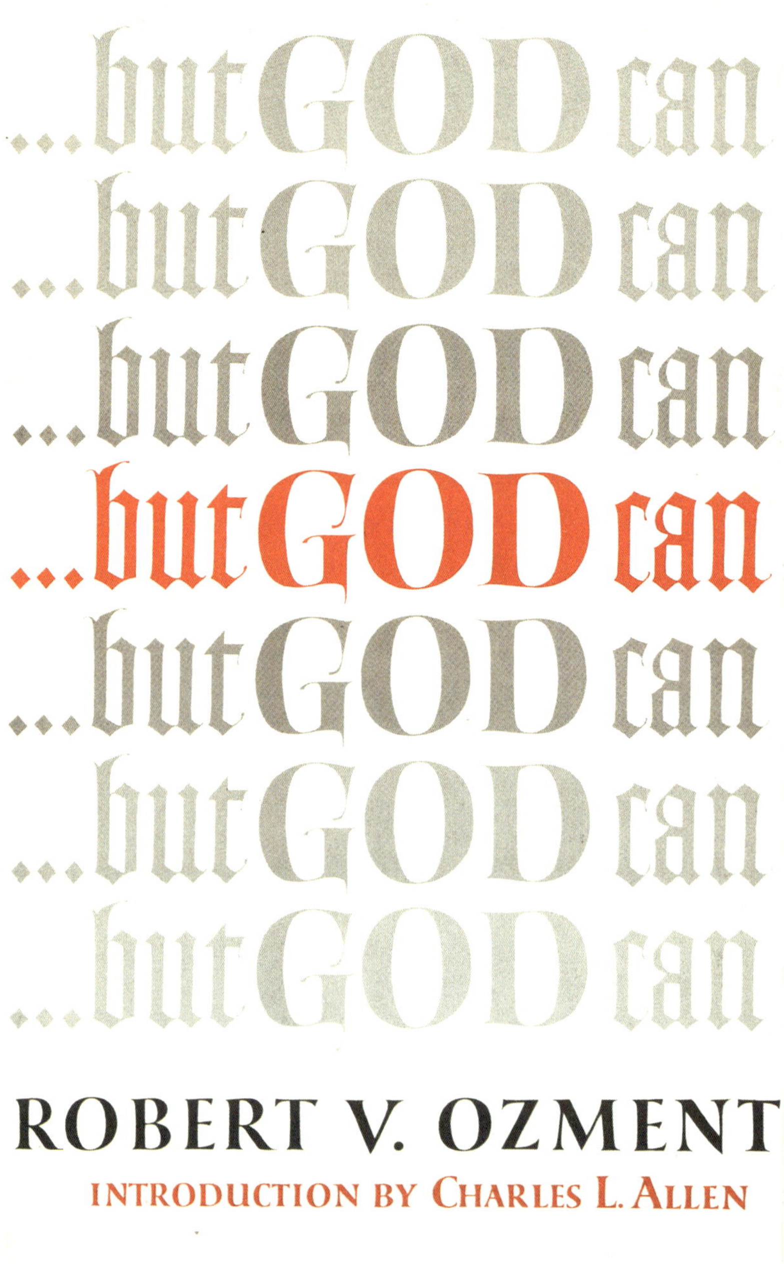

...but GOD can
...but GOD can
...but GOD can
...but GOD can
...but GOD can
...but GOD can
...but GOD can

ROBERT V. OZMENT

INTRODUCTION BY CHARLES L. ALLEN

Repetition often serves as a modern visual metaphor of machine production. Here it is surprisingly effective in conveying a very different message: that of persistent prayer and affirmation of faith.
REVELL, 1962

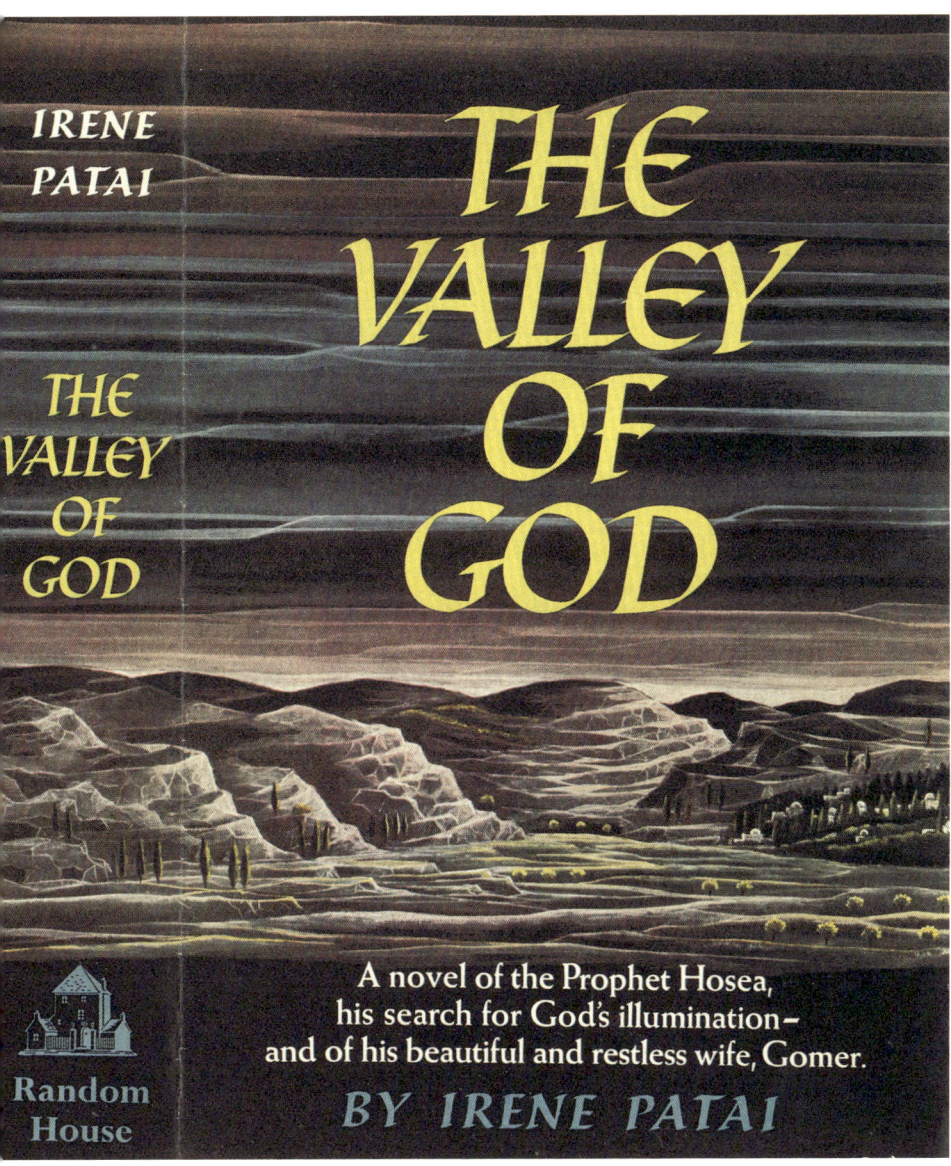

IRENE PATAI

THE
VALLEY
OF
GOD

THE
VALLEY
OF
GOD

Random
House

A novel of the Prophet Hosea,
his search for God's illumination –
and of his beautiful and restless wife, Gomer.

BY IRENE PATAI

The velvet painting color scheme in this design is surprisingly effective in conveying tension and gravity, which creates an apt setting for the life story of the "prophet of doom." RANDOM HOUSE, 1956

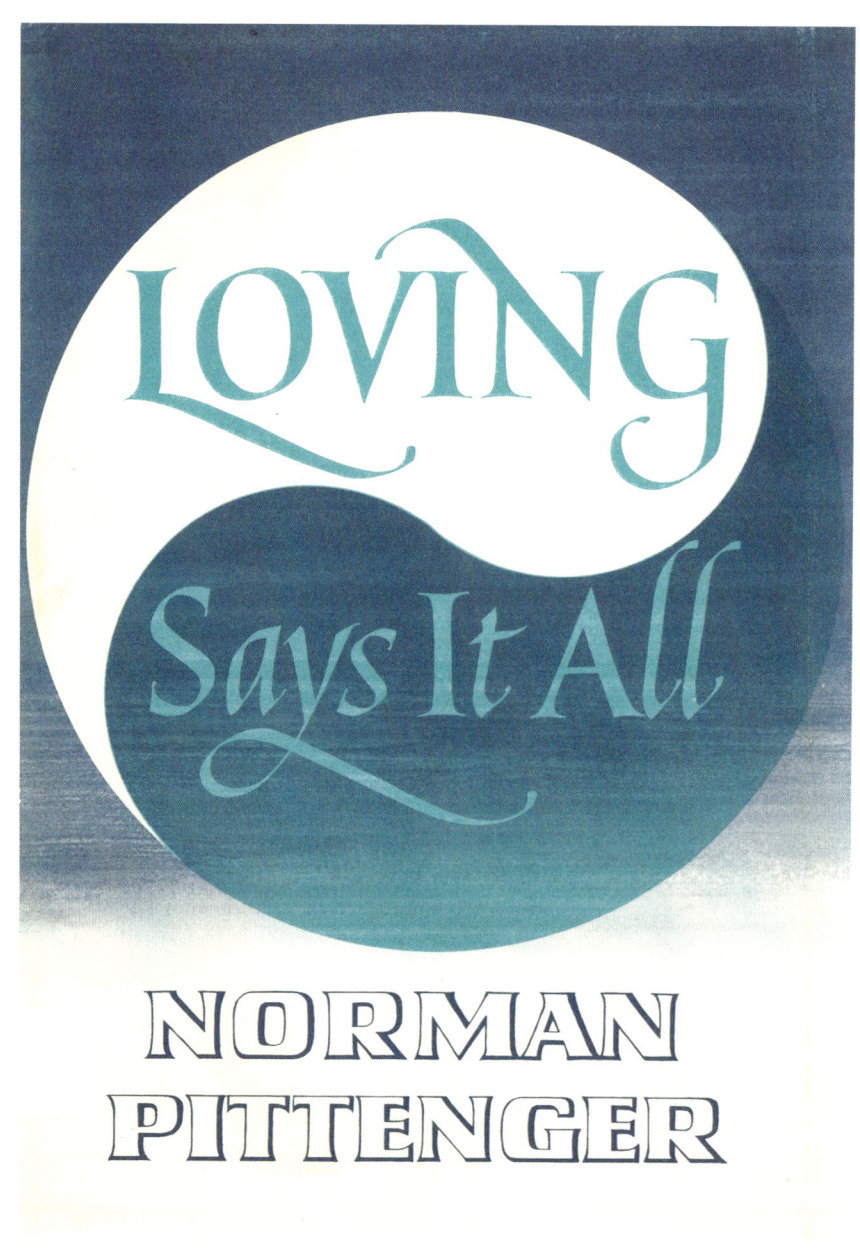

The ancient Taijitu symbol is divested of its cultural allusions and used as an abstraction. The swashes of the lettering echo its shape. PILGRIM PRESS, 1978

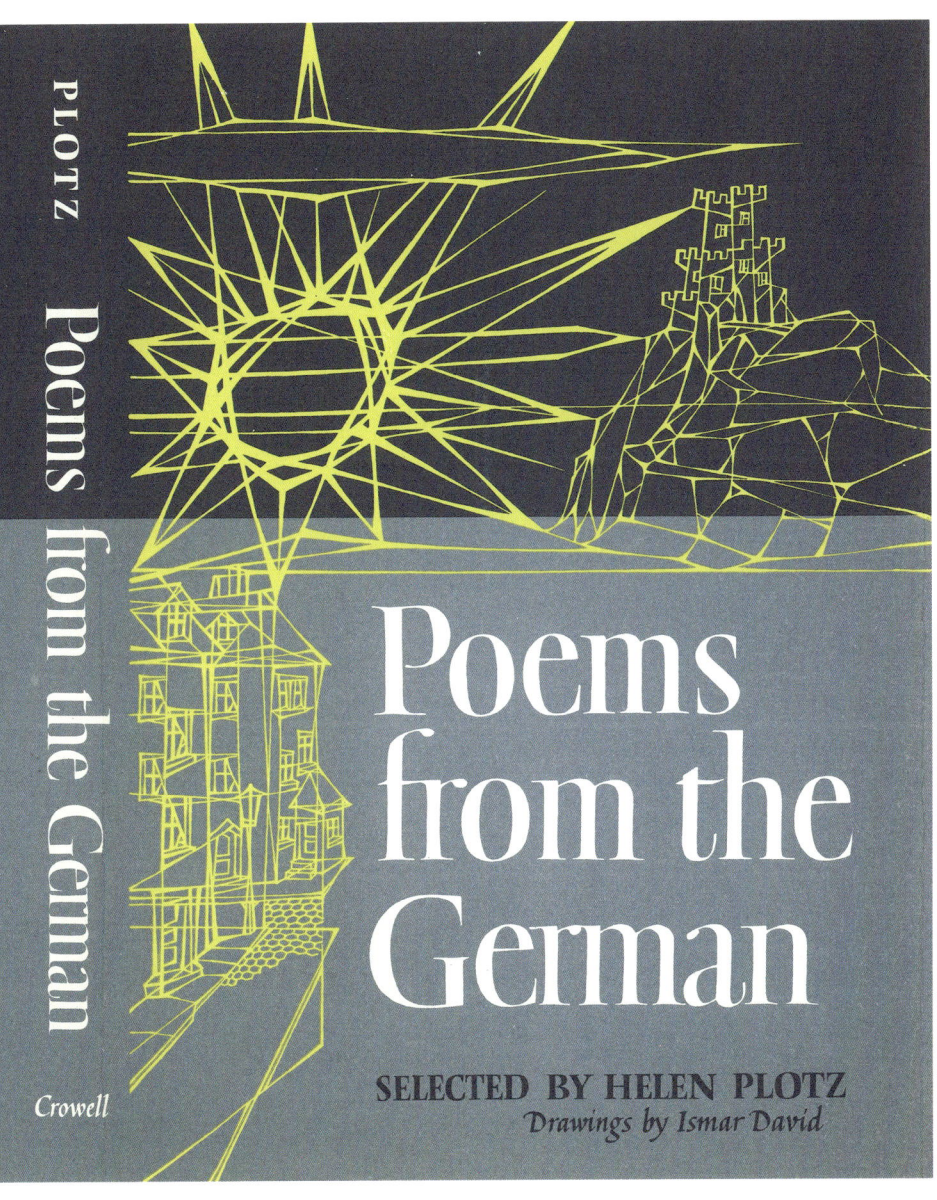

PLOTZ

Poems from the German

Crowell

Poems
from the
German

SELECTED BY HELEN PLOTZ
Drawings by Ismar David

The lettering here hearkens to the modern typography of the nineteenth century, the heyday of German poetry. The illustration refers to the romantic imagery of the same period. Yet, their striking combination is unmistakably contemporary. CROWELL, 1967

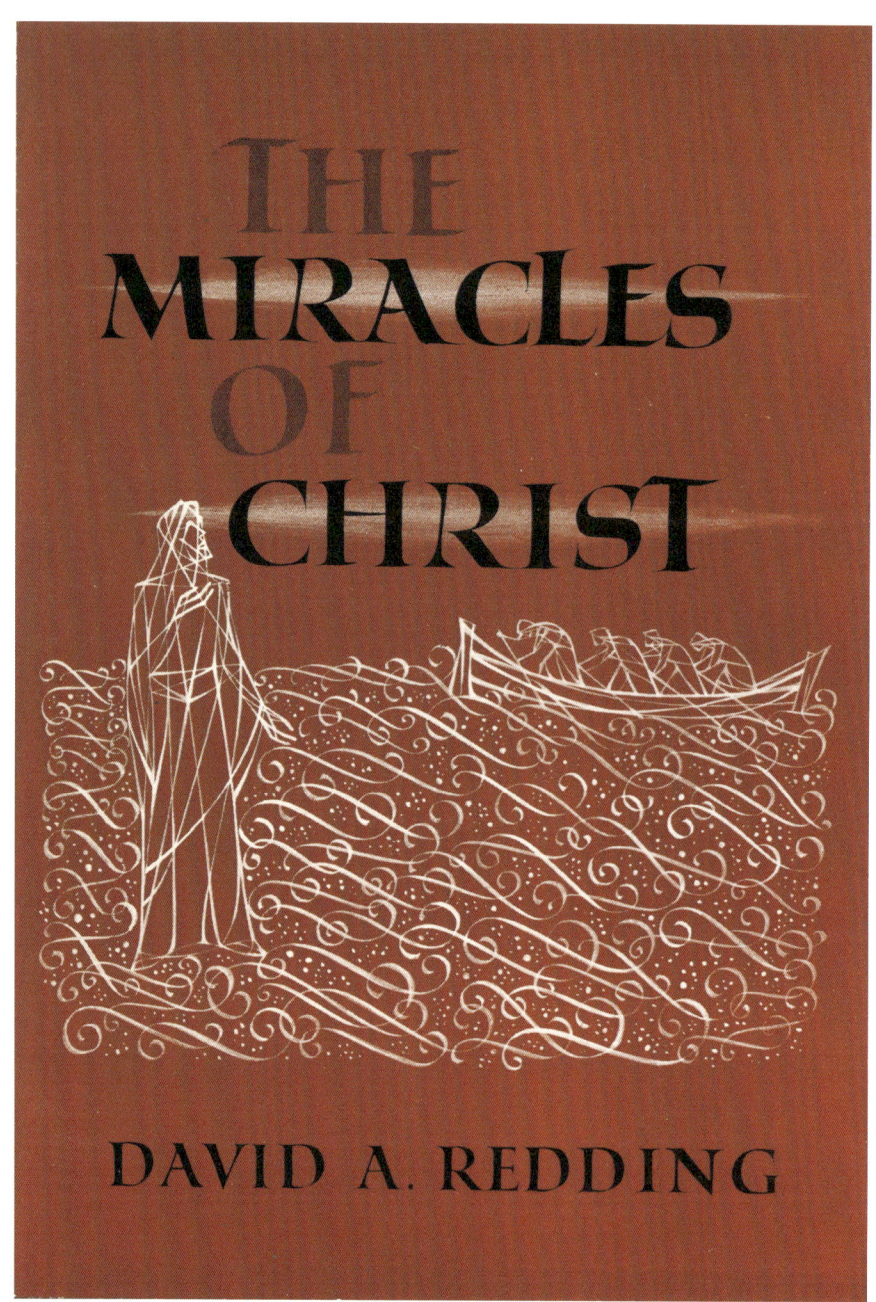

THE MIRACLES OF CHRIST

DAVID A. REDDING

Calligraphic flourishes find their place in the illustration producing a water texture of surprising richness. Black title lettering overprints the light clouds that drop out of the brown background creating a starburst effect. REVELL, 1964

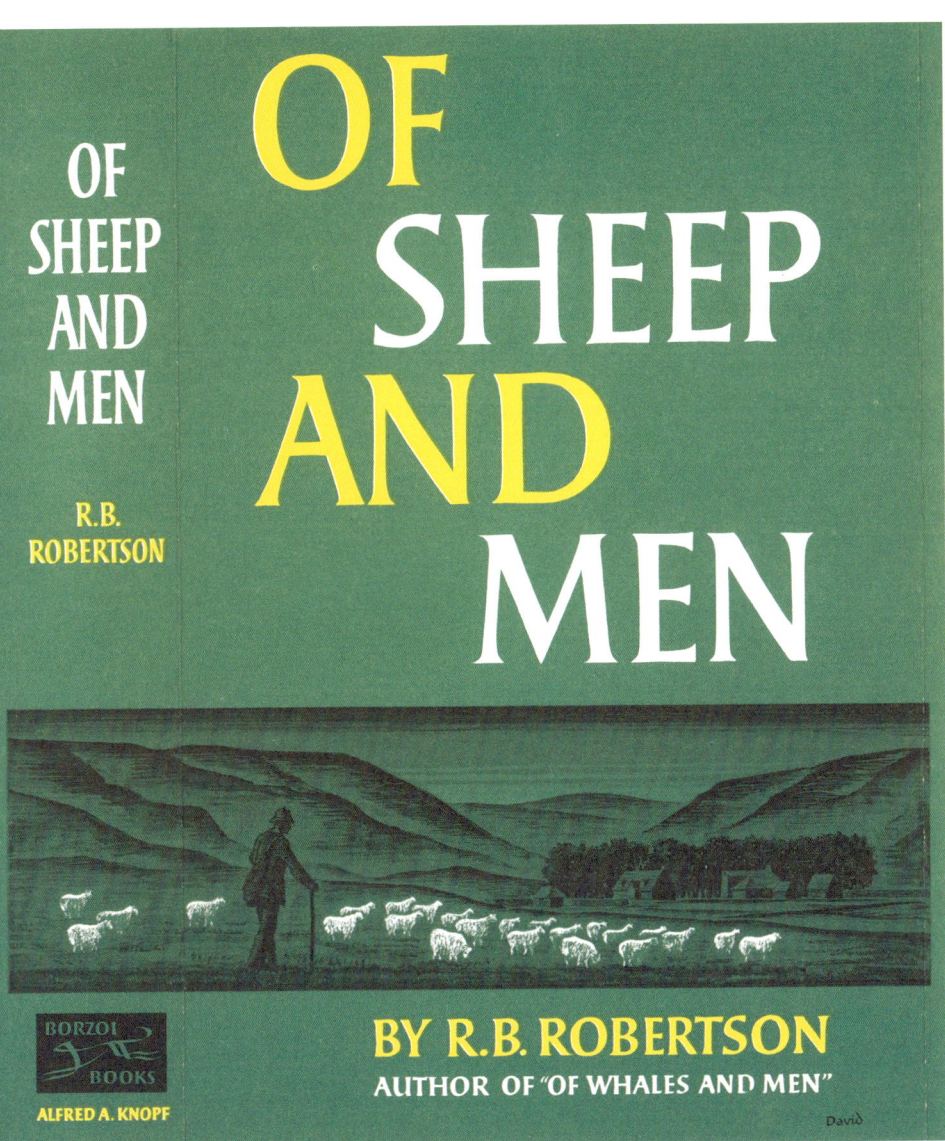

A showcase of the designer's craftsmanship, this jacket is a sequel to an earlier book jacket for *Of Whales and Man* by the same author. The sparse lettering arrangement and the way it integrates with the image is near perfect. The image wraps onto the spine, so that when the section of the book is displayed spine-out, it works both on its own and as part of a larger image. This is an example of mastery with a limited palette, where just three colors are sufficient to create a colorful effect. KNOPF, 1957

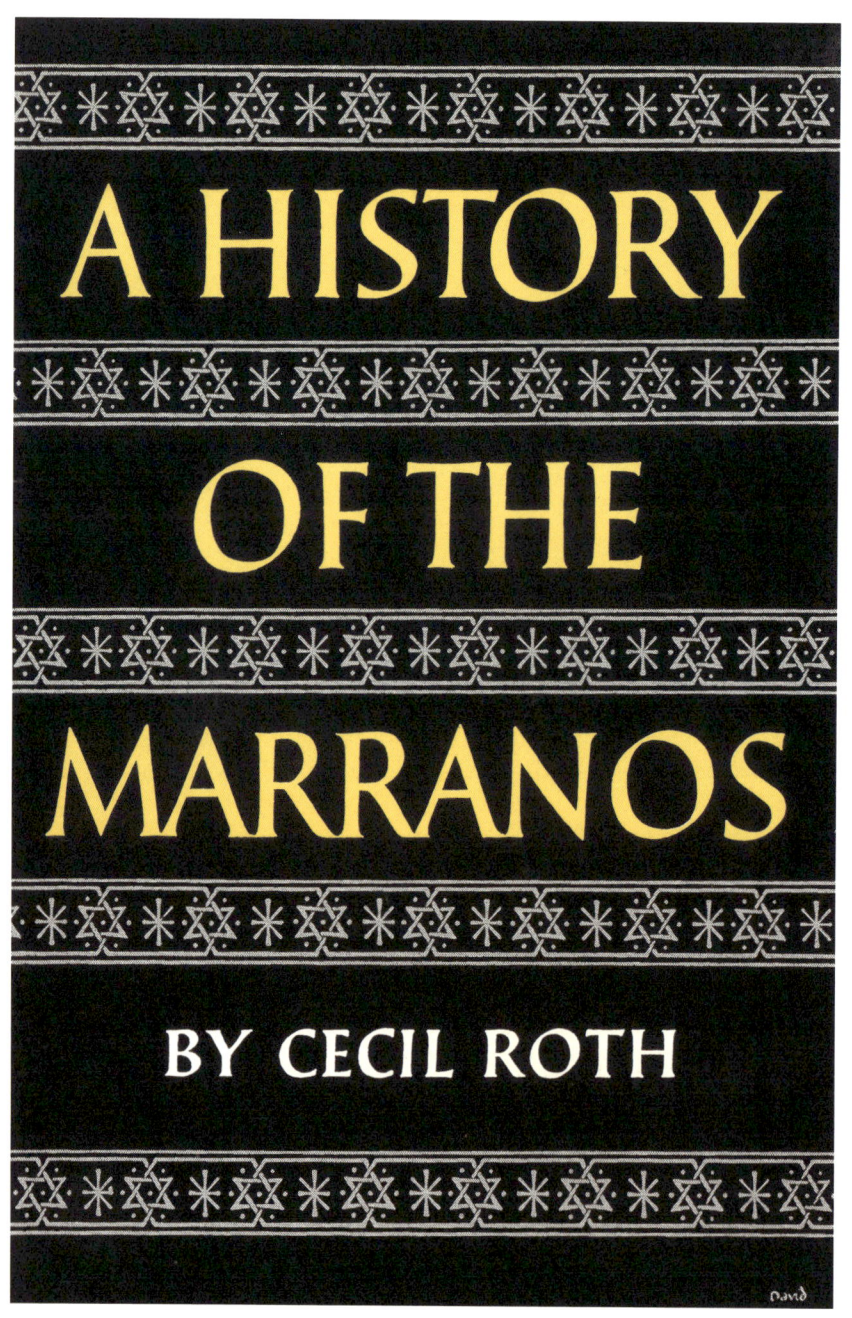

A HISTORY OF THE MARRANOS

BY CECIL ROTH

Occasionally, it is solely the strength of lettering and the beauty of its arrangement, that make the jacket.
JEWISH PUBLICATION SOCIETY OF AMERICA, 1959.

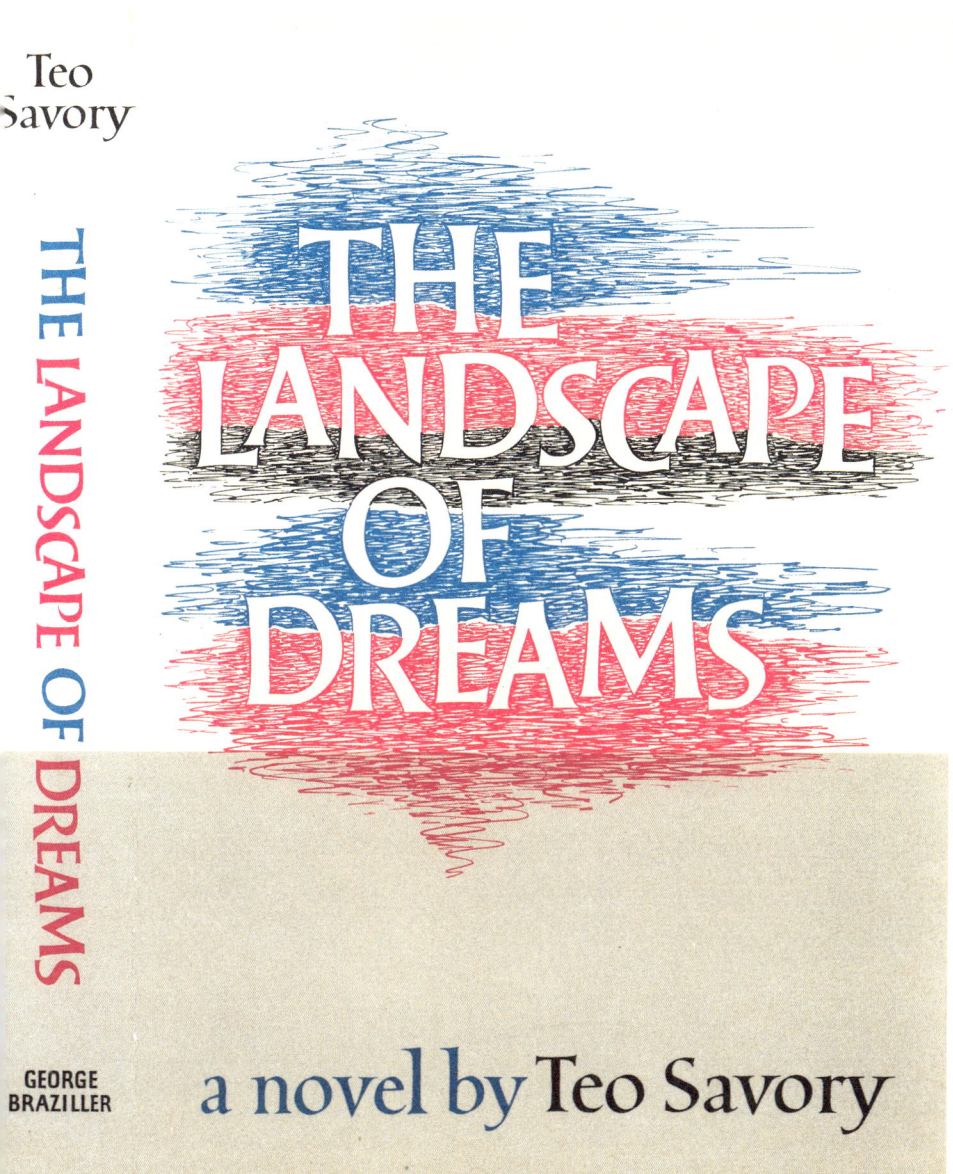

A panel of flat gray tone is sufficient to suggest a landscape and a horizon line. Whimsical, cloud-like shapes denote the sky, while the lettering drops out to the white background, as if to say that dreams are lighter than clouds. BRAZILLER, 1960

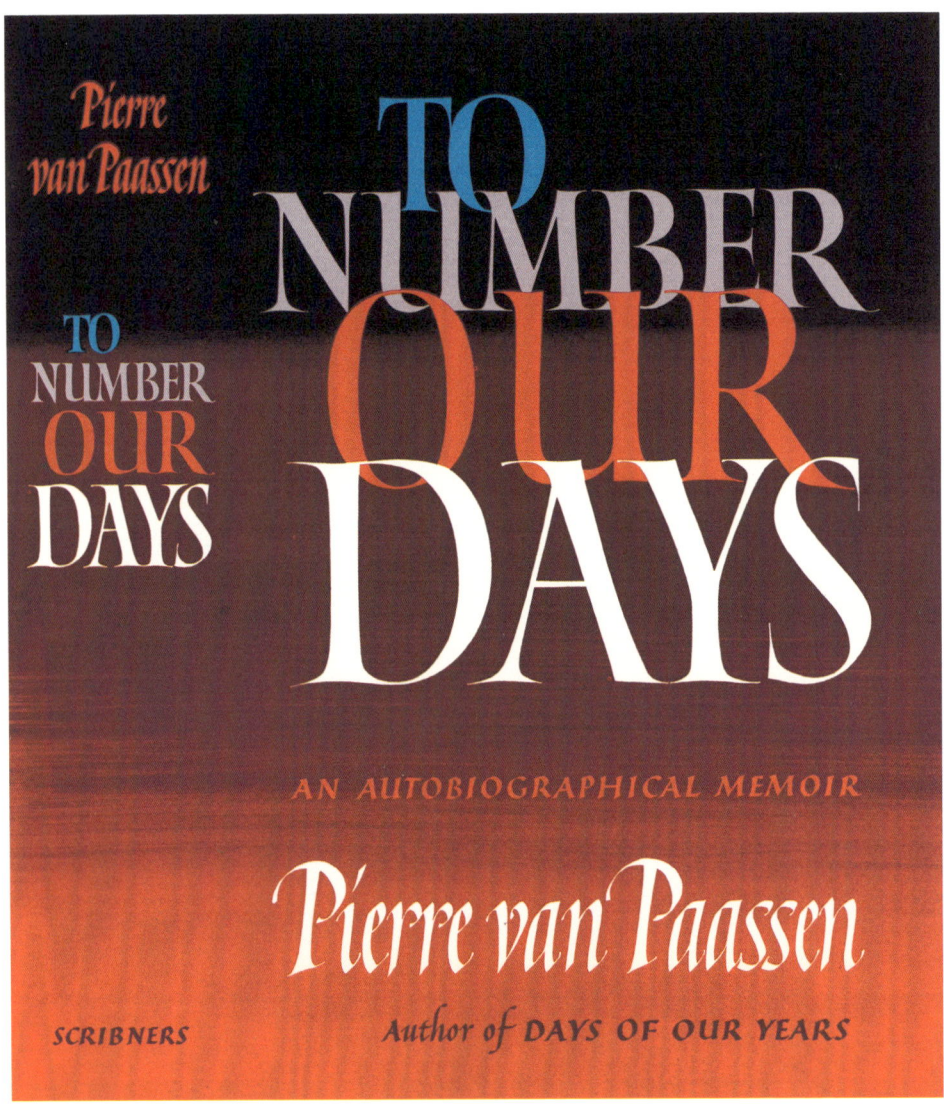

The overlapping lines in this slightly off-center title are superimposed over the plain background that fades into darkness, creating a sense of passing time. The artist achieves his effect with purely abstract means, without the aid of any recognizable symbol or reference. SCRIBNER, 1964

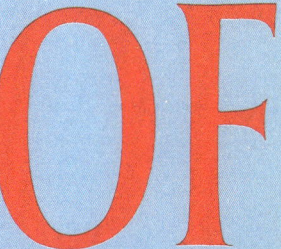

Simon Wolf · Henry Cohen · Edward Israel · Lillian Wald ·

GIANTS

Louis Brandeis · Albert Einstein · Stephen Wise · Henry Monsky ·

OF

**GREAT AMERICAN JEWS
OF THIS CENTURY AND
THEIR CONTRIBUTIONS
TO SOCIAL JUSTICE**

Henrietta Szold · Louis Marshall · Samuel Mayerberg ·

JUSTICE

David Dubinsky · Abraham Cronbach · Herbert Lehman ·

ALBERT VORSPAN

Spine: GIANTS OF JUSTICE — VORSPAN — UAHC

The extensive copy on this jacket is not only organized in a clear and accessible way, but is made attractive.
The names are written in a chancery italic hand that makes them decorative to the point of being ornamental.
A textbook example for the use of hierarchy in design. UNION OF AMERICAN HEBREW CONGREGATIONS, 1960

43

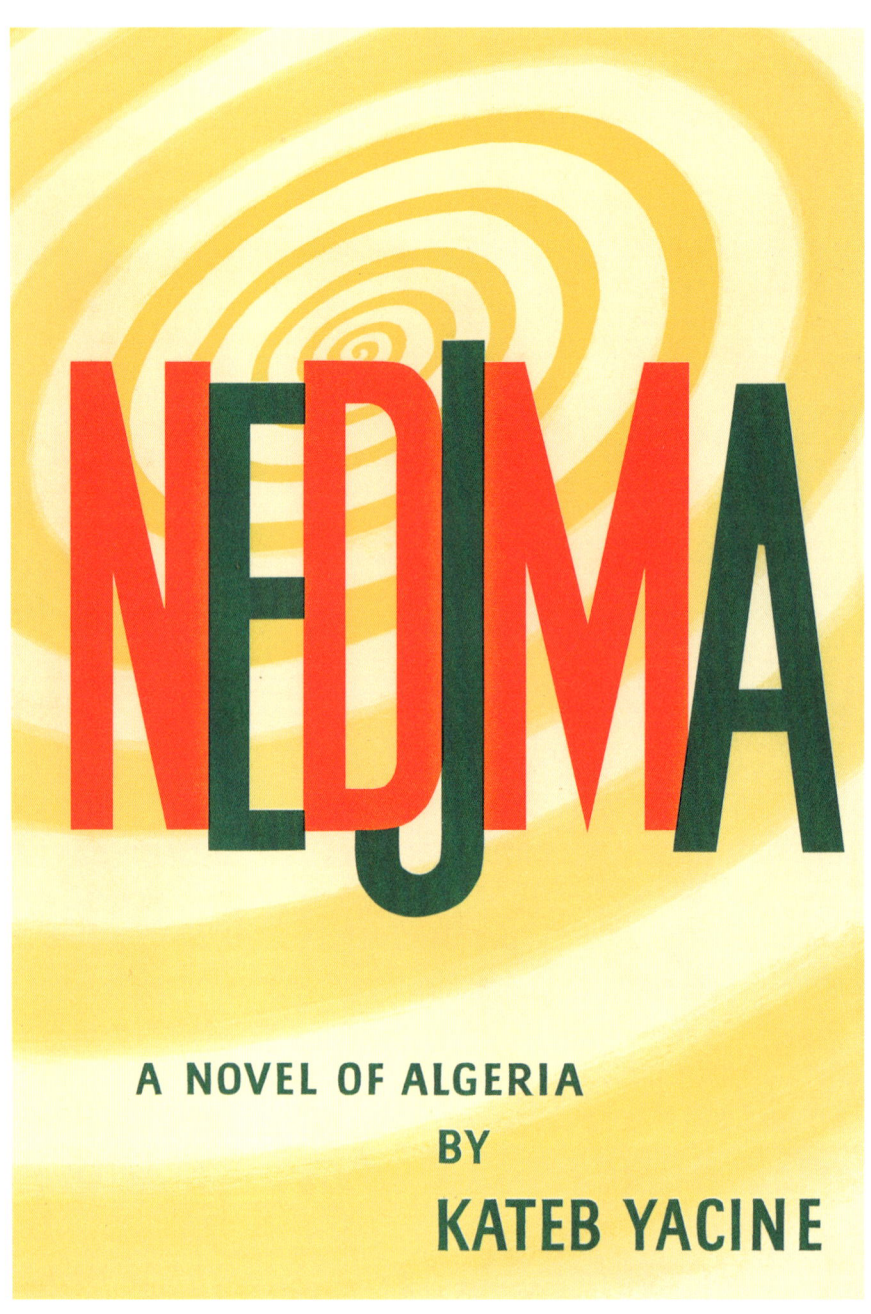

NEDJMA

A NOVEL OF ALGERIA
BY
KATEB YACINE

Perhaps the closest David ever got to modernism, complete with vibrant colors, compressed sans-serif lettering, and an abstract spiral motif. For a traditionalist, this looks remarkably contemporary. BRAZILLER, 1961

The Apostles' Creed for Everyman

WILLIAM BARCLAY

Traditionally centered title lettering is superimposed over an asymmetrical arrangement of abstract shapes, which lends tension to the composition. HARPER & ROW, 1967

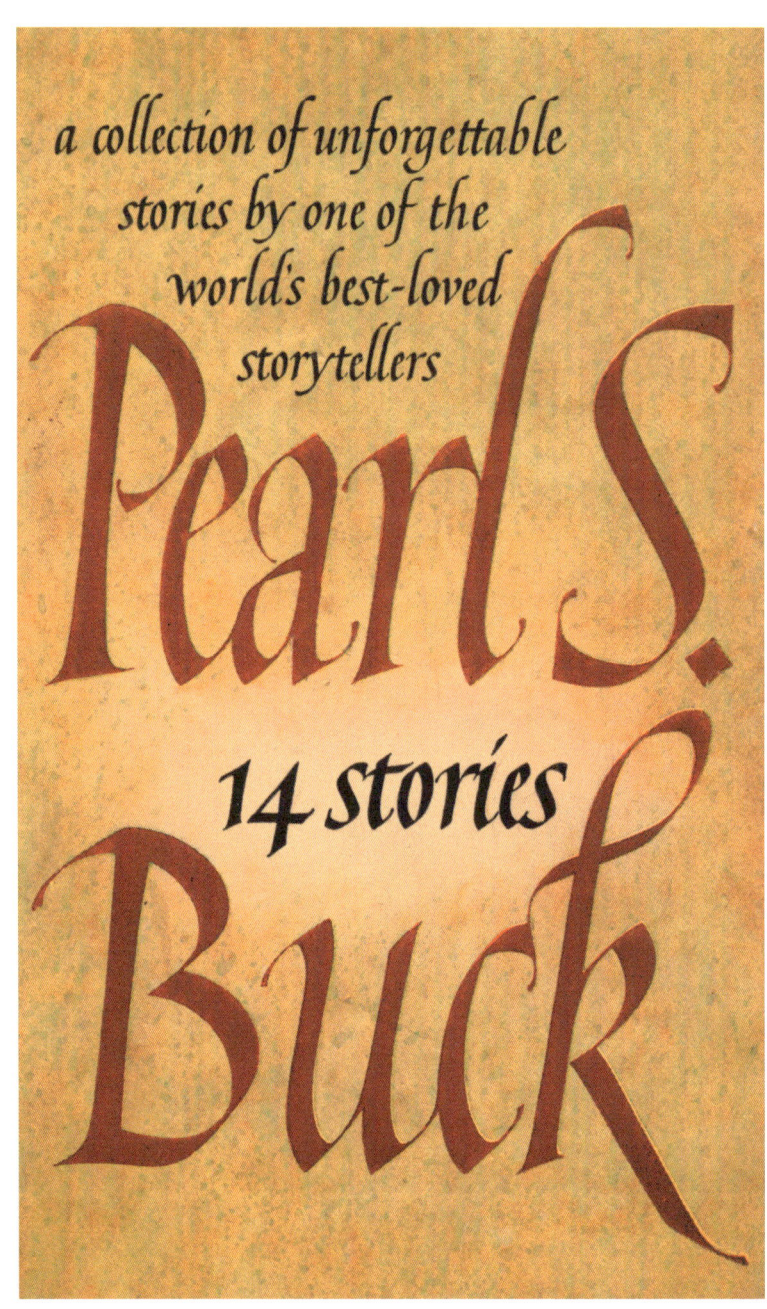

a collection of unforgettable
stories by one of the
world's best-loved
storytellers

Pearl S.

14 stories

Buck

Even when the publisher asks the designer to make the author's name big—really big—as tall
as the whole cover, it may still be done tastefully. POCKET BOOKS, 1963

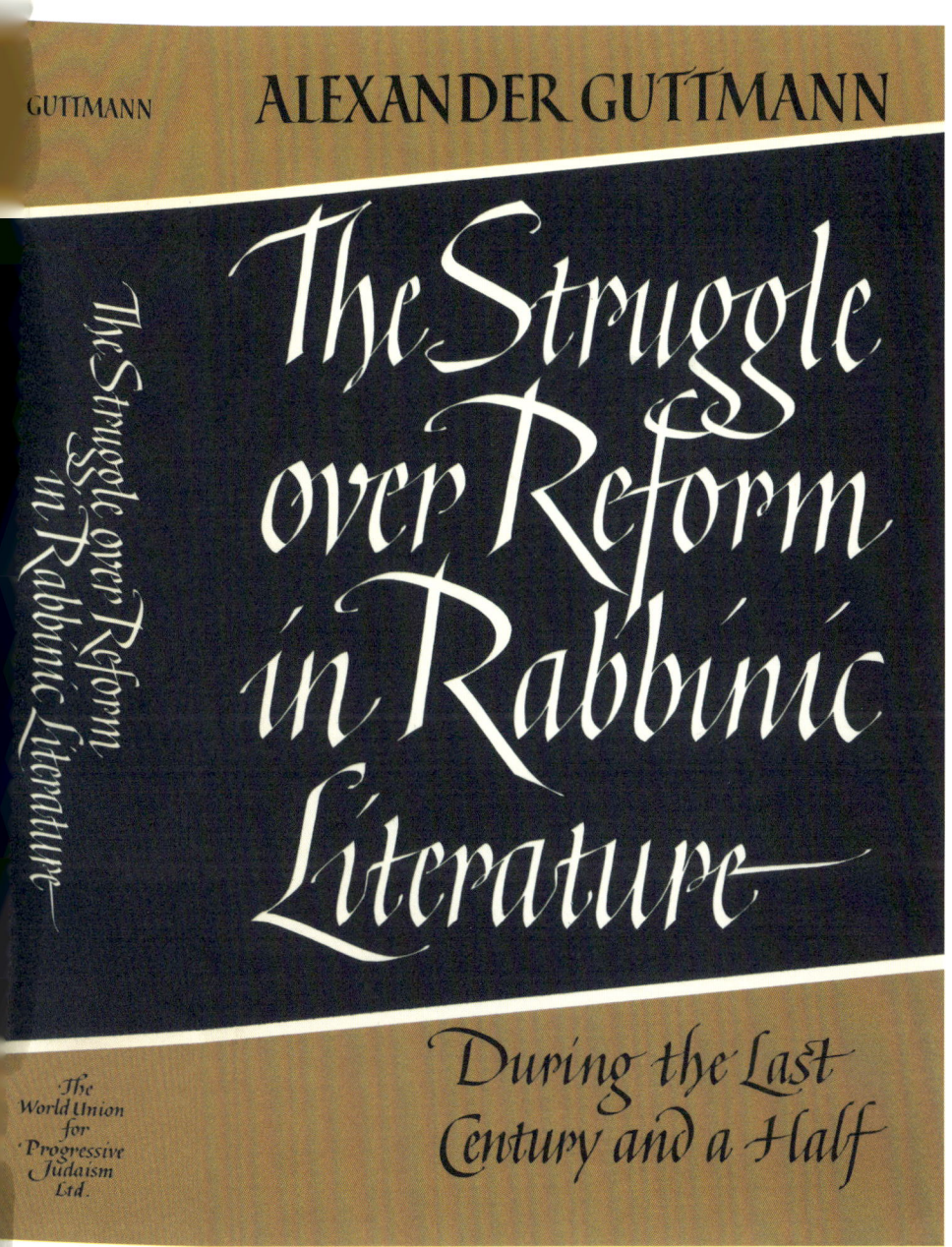

GUTTMANN

ALEXANDER GUTTMANN

The Struggle over Reform in Rabbinic Literature

During the Last Century and a Half

The World Union for Progressive Judaism Ltd.

The uphill slant of the title panel, as well as the energy of the title lettering, lends expressive dynamism to this simple arrangement. WORLD UNION FOR PROGRESSIVE JUDAISM, 1977

Set in Galliard type, with David Classic type on title page.

750 copies printed, of which 250 are reserved for The Typophiles, New York,

as New Series Monograph number 26.

Printed by Thames Printing on Mohawk paper.

Designed by Jerry Kelly.